CHINESE POETRY

AN ANTHOLOGY OF MAJOR MODES AND GENRES

Wai-lim Yip, Editor and Translator

Duke University Press   *Durham and London 1997*

4th printing, 2003

© 1997 Duke University Press

All rights reserved

Printed in the United States of America on acid-free paper ∞

Designed by Mary Mendell

Typeset in Minion at Duke University Press

Library of Congress Cataloging-in-Publication Data appear

on the last printed page of this book.

FOR TZU-MEI

JUNE AND JONAS

CONTENTS

PREFACE TO THE NEW EDITION

Wai-lim Yip

"Wrong from the start!"

Borrowing a phrase from Pound's critique of the decline of English poetic art, in 1960 I protested in dismay and anger against a century of gross distortions of Chinese poetry by translators who allowed the target language (in this case, English) to mask and master the indigenous Chinese aesthetic, creating treacherous modes of representation. These translators seemed unaware that classical Chinese poetry emerges from a perceptual ground with a set of cultural-aesthetic assumptions radically different from that of Western poetry; that its syntax is in many ways inseparable from this perceptual ground; and that by imposing Indo-European linguistic habits on classical Chinese without any adjustment the translators were significantly changing the poetry's perceptual-expressive procedures.

Therefore, in order to remedy these problems in translation, I've organized the Chinese poems in this book into a three-part structure. Given first is the poem in the original Chinese. It is followed by my word-for-word annotations, and, finally, my translation with minimal but workable syntax. I've done this in order to open up an aesthetic space where readers can move back and forth between classical Chinese and modern American perceptual-expressive dimensions.

Underlying the classical Chinese aesthetic is the primary idea of noninterference with Nature's flow. As reflected in poetic language, this idea has engendered freedom from the syntactical rigidities often found in English and most, if not all, of the Indo-European languages. In English, a sentence is almost always structured according to rigid syntactical rules, whereas classical Chinese, as it is used in poetry, is syntactically flexible. For example, although the Chinese language has articles and personal pronouns, they are often dispensed with in poetry. This opens up an indeterminate space for readers to enter and reenter for multiple perceptions rather than locking them into some definite perspectival position or guiding them in a certain direction. Then there is the sparseness, if not absence, of connective elements (prepositions or conjunctions), and this lack, aided by the indeterminancy of parts of speech and no tense declensions in verbs, affords the readers a unique freedom to consort with the objects and events of the real-life world.

The words in a Chinese poem quite often have a loose relationship with readers, who remain in a sort of middle ground between engaging with them (attempting to make predicative connections to articulate relationships between and among the words) and disengaging from them (refraining from doing so, since such predicative acts would greatly restrict the possibility of achieving noninterference). Therefore, the asyntactical and paratactical structures in Chinese poetry promote a kind of prepredicative condition wherein words, like objects (often in a coextensive and multiple montage) in the real world, are free from predetermined relationships and single meanings and offer themselves to readers in an open space. Within this space, and with the poet stepping aside, so to speak, they can move freely and approach the words from a variety of vantage points to achieve different perceptions of the same moment. They have a cinematic visuality and stand at the threshold of many possible meanings.

In retrospect, I must consider myself fortunate to live during a time when both poets and philosophers in the West have already begun to question the framing of language, echoing in part the ancient Taoist critique of the restrictive and distorting activities of names and words and their power-wielding violence, and opening up reconsiderations of language and power, both aesthetically and politically. When Heidegger warns us that any dialogue using Indo-European languages to discuss the spirit of East-Asian poetry will risk destroying the possibility of accurately saying what the dialogue is about, he is sensing the danger of language as a "dwelling," trapping experience within a privileged subjectivity.[1] When William Carlos Williams writes "unless there is / a new mind there cannot be a new / line," he also means "unless there is / a new line there cannot be a new / mind." Until we disarm the tyrannical framing functions of the English language, the natural self in its fullest sentience cannot be released to maximum expressivity. The syntactical innovations initiated by Pound (aided by his discovery of the Chinese character as a medium for poetry), Stein, Williams (who, among other sources, took William James's lesson very seriously, i.e., to retrieve the real existence before it is broken up into serial orders through language and conceptions), and E. E. Cummings, and reinforced in practice and theory by the Black Mountain poets, John Cage, Robert Duncan, and Snyder, suddenly open up a new perceptual-expressive possibility in English, a new ambience whereby I can stage Chinese poetry according to its original operative dynamics rather than tailoring it to fit the Western procrustean bed.[2]

In reprinting this anthology, I wish to make this new perceptual ground and expressive dynamics accessible to more readers who are eager to reach beyond Western frames toward newer landscapes and to enter into an inter-reflective dialogue with Chinese poetry.

1. Martin Heidegger, *On the Way to Language*, trans. Peter D. Hertz (New York: Harper and Row, 1971), pp. 4–5.
2. For a fuller discussion of this change in ambience, see my *Diffusion of Distances: Dialogues between Chinese and Western Poetics* (University of California Press, 1993), especially chapters 2, 3, and 4.

CHINESE POETRY

TRANSLATING CHINESE POETRY

THE CONVERGENCE OF LANGUAGES AND

POETICS—A RADICAL INTRODUCTION*

PART I

Concrete examples before abstractions. First, a short poem by the eighth-century Chinese poet Meng Hao-jan, laid out according to the original order of appearance and graphic impression of the Chinese characters. Beside each character are given word-for-word dictionary annotations plus some bare indications of their grammatical function (i.e., using tentative English classifications). The poem runs:

line 1	移	move (v.)
	舟	boat (n.)
	泊	moor (v.)
	烟	smoke (n./adj.)
	渚	shore (n.)
line 2	日	sun (n.)
	暮	dusk (v.)
	客	traveler (n.)
	愁	grief (n.)
	新	new (adj./v.)
line 3	野	wild/wilderness
	曠	wilderness/far-reaching/empty
	天	sky (n)
	低	low (v./adj.)
	樹	tree/s (n.)

*By "radical" I mean "root." This exploration into Chinese and comparative poetics is an outgrowth and theoretical extension of some of the aesthetic positions implied in my earlier works, among them, *Ezra Pound's Cathay* (Princeton, 1969), *Phenomenon, Experience, Expression* (text in Chinese [Hong Kong, 1969]) and an essay titled "Aesthetic Perception in Classical Chinese Poetry" in *Chung-hua wen-hua fu-hsing yueh-k'an* (*Chinese Cultural Renaissance Monthly*, vol. 4, no. 5 [Taipei, May 1, 1971], pp. 8–13).

line 4 江 river (n.)
清 clear (adj.)
月 moon (n)
近 near (v./adj.)
人 man (n.)

How is an English reader to respond to this poem? I mean by an English reader one whose language habits are those that demand rigid syntactical cooperation between and among parts of speech, such as: a subject leads to a verb to an object; articles govern certain nouns; past actions cast in past tenses; third person singular asks for a change in verb endings, etc. How is he to respond to a poem written in a language in which such rigid syntactical demands are sparse, if not absent? Is he to supply some of the missing links between the characters? This is perhaps the first question any reader will attempt to answer. Many readers and translators simply go ahead and do it without reflecting a bit whether such an act is legitimate, aesthetically speaking. Before examining closely some of these attempts, it is perhaps useful for us to see the degree of syntactical freedom open to the user of the classical Chinese language. Let us use an emphatic example, a palindrome by Su Tung-p'o (1036–1101). This is a seven-character, eight-line regulated poem which can be read backward with different meaning. One line from this poem should suffice:

a.			b.		
tide/s	潮		pour-fall	傾	
follow	隨		mountain/s	山	
dark	暗		snow	雪	
wave/s	浪		wave/s	浪	
snow	雪		dark	暗	
mountain/s	山		follow	隨	
pour-fall	傾		tide/s	潮	

a. Tide/s pursue dark waves, snow mountain/s fall
b. Mountain-pouring snow-waves darkly follow tides

The line reads forward and backward perfectly naturally. To do this in English is unimaginable. The examples in English such as "Madam, I'm Adam" and "Able was I ere I saw Elba" are not really doing what the Chinese language can do. Translated into English, the syntactical demands (precise grammatical function alloted to each word) become obvious. Which brings us to conclude that the Chinese language can easily be free from syntactical bounds, although one must hasten to add that this does not mean Chinese is without syntax. This freedom from syntactical rigidity, while it no doubt creates tremendous problems for the translator, provides the user with a unique mode of presentation. (Or perhaps we should say it is the unique mode of perception of reality of the Chinese which has occasioned this flexibility of syntax.) Try two lines by Tu Shen-yen (between seventh and eighth centuries):

1.1			1.2		
cloud/s	雲		plum/s	梅	
mist/s	霞		willow/s	柳	
go-out	出		cross	渡	
sea	海		river	江	
dawn	曙		spring	春	

Are we to read these lines as:

Clouds and mists move out *to* the sea *at* dawn
Plums and willows across the river *bloom in* spring.

There is something distorted in this version when compared to the original order of impressions. What about reading them in the following manner.

Clouds and mists
Out to sea:
Dawn

Plums and willows
Across the river:
Spring

And on aesthetic grounds, what kind of perception has this order of words promoted? This leads us to an exploration of some of the central questions of Chinese poetics.

Returning to Meng Hao-jan's poem, we can now ask some more specific questions: Who moves the boat to moor by the smoke-shore? How are we to arbitrate this? Shall we assume, as with most of our Chinese translators, that the speaker "I" is always crouched behind the poetic statement or image? What is the difference between putting the "I" into the poem and not putting it there? Is it possible not to have the personal pronoun? To have it thus is to specify the speaker or agent of the action, restricting the poem, at least on the linguistic level, to one participant only, whereas freedom from the personal pronoun universalizes the state of being or feeling, providing a scene or a situation into which all the readers would move, as it were, to take part directly.

This poem contains a number of actions. Actions take place in time, but the classical Chinese language is tense*less*. Why tense*less*? Shall we cast these actions into the past, as evidenced by some of the following examples? The fact is: if the Chinese poet has avoided restricting actions to one specific agent, he has also refrained from committing them to finite time. (Or shall we say, the mental horizon of the Chinese poets does not lead them to posit an event within a segment of finite time.) The past, present and future tenses in Indo-European languages set time and space limits even on the linguistic level, but the Chinese verbs (or verb elements) tend to return to Phenomenon itself, that undifferentiated mode of being, *which is timeless, the concept of time being a human invention arbitrarily imposed upon Phenomenon.*

We have seen the ambiguous grammatical roles some Chinese characters can play. In this poem, two verbs in line 3 and 4 assume, as it were, a double identity. How are we to determine the syntactical relation between the objects before or after "low" or "lowers" and "near" or "nears?" Is it the vastness of the wilderness that has lengthened the sky, lowering it to the trees, or does the breadth of the stretch of the trees seem to pull the sky to the wilderness? If we read the word 低 (low) not as a verb, but as an adjective, the line becomes three visual units: vast wilderness/sky/low trees. What choice are we to make, which syntactical relation should we determine? Or should we determine at all?

Enough exposition has now been given to the multiple levels of possibilities for the poem as enhanced by flexible syntax and other unique features of the Chinese language. The questions I pose here are not for mere grammatical exercise; they are reflected as critical problems in many examples of translations. (Italicized words indicate the translator's insertion to supply what he believes to be the missing links; words in bold type indicate the translator's interpretation or paraphrase of the original images):

Giles (1898):
    I steer *my* boat to anchor
        by the mist-clad river eyot
    And **mourn** *the* dying day *that brings me*
        nearer to my fate.
    Across the woodland wild *I see*
        the sky **lean on** the trees,
    While close to hand the *mirror* moon
        floats on the shining streams.[1]

Fletcher (1919):
    Our boat *by the* mist-covered islet we ti*ed.*
    The sorrows *of absence* the sunset *brings* back.
    Low breasting the foliage the sky loomed black.
    The river *is* bright *with the* moon at our side.[2]

Bynner (1920):
    While my little boat moves on its mooring mist,
    And **daylight wanes, old memories begin. . . .**
    How wide the world was, how close the trees to heaven!
    And how clear in the water the nearness of the moon![3]

---

1. *Selected Chinese Verses*, trans. by Herbert A. Giles and Arthur Waley (Shanghai, 1934), p. 22. This book consists of two parts: poems translated by Giles and those by Waley. It offers a good chance for comparison of the styles of these two early translators.

2. W. J. B. Fletcher, *More Gems of Chinese Poetry* (Shanghai, 1919), p. 150.

3. Witter Bynner, *The Jade Mountain* (New York, 1929). The poem can be located conveniently in the paperback edition (Anchor, 1964), p. 85.

Christy (1929):

> *At* dusk *I* moored *my* boat *on* the banks of the river;
> With the oncoming of night **my friend** is depress*ed*;
> **Heaven itself seems to cover over the gloomy trees
>   of the wide fields.**
> **Only** the moon, shining on the river, is near man.[4]

Jenyns (1944):

> *I* move *my* boat and anchor in the mists *off* an islet;
> With the setting sun the traveler's heart grows
>   melancholy once more.
> **On every side is a desolate expanse of water;**
> **Somewhere** the sky comes down to the trees
> And the clear water **reflects** a neighboring moon.[5]

Other experimental attempts: [6]

(a) Moving boat, mooring, smoke-shore.
    Sun darkening: new sadness of traveler.
    Wilderness, sky lowering trees.
    Limpid river: moon nearing man.

(b) Boat moves to moor mid shore-smoke.
    Sun sinks. Traveler feels fresh sadness.
    Wilderness
                    Sky
                        Low trees
                            Limpid river
Moon nears man.

(c) A boat slows, moors by beach-run in smoke.
    Sun fades: a traveler's sorrow freshens.
    Open wilderness.
    Wide sky.
    A stretch of low trees.
    Limpid river.
    Clear moon close to man.

---

4. Arthur Christy, *Images in Jade* (New York, 1929), p. 74.

5. Soame Jenyns, *A Further Selection from the Three Hundred Poems of the T'ang Dynasty* (London, 1944), p. 76.

6. These versions were done in a workshop by my students in a seminar on the theory and practice of translation, University of California, San Diego.

Reading all the above translations against the original with which we are now familiar (I will not comment on the experimental versions; they are here for contrast and will figure in my argument later), we find that they are secondary elaborations of some primary form of experience, the unfolding of some schemata into separate parts. All the translators, starting with Giles, must have been led by the sparseness of syntax in the original to believe that the Chinese characters must be telegraphic—in the sense that they are shorthand signs for a longhand message—and so they took it as their task to translate the shorthand into longhand, poetry into prose, adding commentary all along to aid understanding, not knowing that these are "pointers" toward a finer shade of suggestive beauty which the discursive, analytical, longhand unfolding process destroys completely. The fact is: these images, often coexisting in spatial relationships, form an atmosphere or environment, an ambience, in which the reader may move and be directly present, poised for a moment before being imbued with the atmosphere that evokes (*but does not state*) an aura of feeling (in this case, grief), a situation in which he may participate in completing the aesthetic experience of an intense moment, the primary form of which the poet has arrested in concrete data.

It is obvious that we cannot approach this poem and most other Chinese poems with the arbitrary time categories of the West, based as they are on a causal linearity imposed by human conceptualization. The Western concept of *being* conceals *being* rather than exposing it; it turns us away from the appeal of the concreteness of objects and events in Phenomenon rather than bringing us into immediate contact with them. The capacity of the Chinese poem to be free from Western arbitrary temporal constructs and to keep a certain degree of close harmony with the concrete events in Phenomenon, can be illustrated by the way film handles temporality, for film is a medium most felicitous in approximating the immediacy of experience. Without mulling over the complex use of time and space in the art of film, let us get down to the fundamentals. For our purpose, a passage from Stephenson-Debrix's introductory book, *The Cinema as Art* (Penguin, 1969), will make this clear. Cinema has:

> a natural freedom in temporal construction. . . . the lack of time prepositions and conjunctions, tenses and other indications. . . . can leave the film free to reach the spectator with an immediacy which literature is unable to match. [p. 107]

Time prepositions and conjunctions such as *"Before* he came . . . *since* I have been here . . . *then* . . ."* do not exist in a film, nor do they in actual events in life. No tense in either case. "When we watch a film, it is just something that is happening—now" (p. 100).

Similarly, the Chinese line

野　曠　天　低　樹
vast-plains　sky　　low　tree

when translated into "As the plain is vast, the sky lowers the trees," immediately loses its cinematic visuality promoted by what I once called "spotlighting activity"[7] or what the filmmakers called "mobile point of view" of the spectator, loses the acting-out of the objects, the *now*ness and the concreteness of the moment. (By this example, I do not mean to imply that the Chinese do not have time-indicators at all. They do, but they are often avoided, aided by the flexibility of syntax.) We can now see that the experimental versions of this line, in their somewhat naive way (i.e., viewed from the cultural burden of the English language), have perhaps brought back more of this cinematic directness of the moment.

(1)   Wilderness
           Sky
                 Low trees

(2)   Open wilderness.
       Wide sky.
       A stretch of low trees.

and the approximation of Tu Shen-yen's lines into:

Clouds and mists
     Out to sea:
           Dawn

Plums and willows
     Across the river:
           Spring

is perhaps not entirely out of order.

Much of the art of Chinese poetry lies in the way in which the poet captures the visual events as they emerge and act themselves out before us, releasing them from the restrictive concept of time and space, letting them leap out directly from the undifferentiated mode of existence instead of standing between the reader and the events explaining them, analyzing them. To say that the Chinese have no time and space categories or to say that Chinese poetry has no place for commentary would be overstating the case, but it is also true that they are infrequently and seldom extensively used. They would not force the perspective of the ego as a means of ordering the Phenomenon before them. The lack of the use of personal pronouns is not just some "curious habit of mind"; it is in tune with the Chinese concept of losing yourself in the flux of events, the Way (Tao), the million changes constantly happening before us.[8]

---

7. See my *Ezra Pound's Cathay*, pp. 38, 147–148, 159–162 or my *Modern Chinese Poetry* (Iowa, 1970), "Introduction."
8. Commenting on Chuang Tzu's idea of change, the Kuo Hsiang text (third century A.D.) has this to say: "The sage roams in the path of a million changes—a million things, a million changes—and thus, he changes in accordance with the law of a million changes." And the Taoist-oriented neo-Confucianist

With this perspectivism in our mind, we can now understand more fully the asyntactical or paratactical formation of many of the Chinese lines.

First, a normal syntactical type that most resembles the English subject-verb-object structure:

(A) s-v-o

a.

孤 燈 燃 客 夢
寒 杵 搗 鄉 愁
　　　　岑參：客舍

lone/lamp/burn/ traveler('s)/dream
cold/pounding-stick-/pound/home/-sickness
　　　(for-washing-clothes)
—Tsen Ts'an (graduated 744)

b.

雲 迎 出 塞 馬
風 捲 渡 河 旗
　　　沈佺期：送友人北征

cloud(s)/receive/go-out-of-the-Pass (adj.)/horse
wind(s)/roll/crossing-the-river (adj.)/flag
—Shen Ch'uan-chi (d. ca. 713)

There is little difficulty in reading and translating lines of this structure into English, except for the usual consideration of the correct choice of words. The examples of asyntactical or paratactical lines which abound in Chinese poetry are the

---

Shao Yung (1011–1077), in the introduction to his collection of poems "Beat the Earthen Chime," elaborates from Lao Tzu the following view that has dominated Chinese art and literature since early times:

. . . the one:
　　to view Human Nature through the Way
　　Mind through Human Nature
　　Body through Mind
　　Things through Body
　　(Control, yes, there is,
　　But not free from harm)

Is unlike the other:
　　to view the Way through the Way
　　Human Nature through Human Nature
　　Mind through Mind
　　Body through Body
　　Things through Things
　　(even if harm were intended,
　　Can it be done?)

8

ones that trouble the English (and European) translators the most. And it is here the perspectivism outlined above can easily come to our aid. Let us look at some concrete examples:

(B) Phase I—Phase II (and sometimes Phase III)

a. 星 臨 萬 戶 動　杜甫：春宿左省
star(s)/come/ten-thousand/house(s)/move
—Tu Fu (712–770)

Compare it with:

> While the stars are twinkling above the ten-thousand
> households. . . . [9]
> —William Hung

The translation here has changed the visual events into *statements about* these visual events. "Stars come" could perhaps be interpreted as temporal, but it is time spatialized, which is what an event means: an event *takes* (time) *place* (space). But when "while" is added, the translator ignores the inseparability of time and space. Similarly, in the line:

月 落 烏 啼 霜 滿 天
　　　　張繼：楓橋夜泊

moon/set/crow(s)/caw/frost/full/sky
(Moondown: crows caw. Frost, a skyful)
—Chang Chi (graduated 753)

"Moondown" is at once a space-fact and a time-fact in the form of a visual event. Hence, when rendered into "As the moon sets," etc., the significance and the concreteness of the event is relegated to a subordinate position. Consider not only the visuality of the event but also the independence of each visual event, so as to promote a kind of spatial tension among, and coexistence with, the other visual events. To translate these lines:

星 垂 平 野 闊
月 湧 大 江 流
　　　　杜甫：旅夜書懷

star(s)/dangle/flat/plain/broad(ens)
moon/surge(s)/big/river/flow(s)
—Tu Fu

---

9. William Hung, *Tu Fu: China's Greatest Poet* (Cambridge, Mass., 1952), p. 105.

into

> The stars lean down from open space
> And the moon comes running up the river
> —Bynner [10]

> Stars drawn low by the vastness of the plain.
> The moon rushing forward in the river's flow.
> —Birch [11]

is to ignore the spatial coexistence of these events and, in doing so, the translat- ors have denied the capacity of the reader-viewer to move in among them—even though one still finds great beauty in the translated lines—beauty of a different order of impressions from the original. Equally significant is the order of appear- ance of these visual events. The order of noticing—in Meng Hao-jan's poem (like the camera-movement), first the "vast wilderness," then moving backward to in- clude the "sky" within our ken before zooming in upon the "low trees"—mim- ics the activities of our perceiving act, hence enabling the reader-viewer to relive the life of the poetic moment. Measuring this against the translations of this line given earlier, the loss is too obvious to need comment here. Similarly, we allow the fol- lowing version of the line "moon/surges/big/river/flows" (noticing gleaming brightness before noticing movement of the river) into "Le Grand Fleuve s'écoule, aux remous de la lune"[12] only at the risk of falsifying the authenticity of the life of the moment. We can see here that poets whose perceptual horizons emphasize the miming of the activities of the perceiving act by tuning the visual events according to the gradations of color and light in the total makeup of the growth of the mo- ment, poets such as Wang Wei (701–761) and Meng Hao-jan, suffer the most in English translations. Let us look at just one such violation:

空　山　　不見人
Empty/mountain/not/see/man
—Wang Wei

becomes, in Bynner's hand,

> There seems to be no one on the empty mountain.[13]

The analytical or explanatory "There seems to be no one" represents, of course, the translator's interference in the direct contact of the "empty mountain" with the viewer-reader, and to put "no one" ahead of "empty mountain" violates the life of the moment: we notice the *emptiness,* the *openness* first before we are aware of the other state of being.

10. Bynner, *The Jade Mountain,* p. 122.
11. Birch, ed., *An Anthology of Chinese Literature* (New York, 1965), p. 238.
12. The translation is by Tch'eng Ki-hien and J. Dieny. See Paul Demieville, ed., *Anthologie de la poésie*
13. Bynner, *The Jade Mountain,* p. 153.

Wang Wei is prized for his ability to turn language into miming gestures of the perceiving act. It is instructive to scan a few examples. I offer here very literal renderings, for illustrative purposes:

White clouds—looking back—close up
Green mists—entering to see—nothing

There are changing perspectives in these lines: "white clouds" (shot one, from a distance): "looking back" (shot two, viewer coming out from opposite direction, turning his head back) "close up" (shot three, viewer retiring to same position as shot one). The visual events are accentuated the way a mimer, in order to reflect an event that is not visible, forms gestures and moments, highlighting them to suggest the energy flow that originally supports that event. Arne Zaslove, in a demonstration-lecture in The Project of Music Experiment at the University of California, San Diego, in January 1973, gave an example that articulates the curve of energy flow of the moment most clearly. He said:

> Supposing a man is carrying a heavy suitcase with both of his hands. (He proceeds to place both of his hands on the imaginary handle and lift the imaginary heavy suitcase.) You will find that your whole body has to bend sideways toward your right to balance off the weight. If the mimer should at this point bend toward the left, the whole miming act is false and becomes unrecognizable.

Words, as signs, function at the maximum when they capture the life-mechanism of the moment of experience in ways similar to those described by Zaslove. In Wang Wei, Li Po (701–762), Li Shang-yin (812?–858) and many others, the tendency is to reproduce visual curves of the events, emphasizing different phases of perception with a mobile point of view or spotlighting activities. Here are some more examples that need no further comment:

大漠　孤烟　直
Vast desert: lone smoke, straight
—Wang Wei

孤帆遠影碧空盡
(A) lone sail, (a) distant shade, lost into the blue horizon
    [literally: blue/sky/end (v.)]
—Li Po

沧 海 月 明 珠 有 泪

Dark sea. Bright moon. Pearls with tears
—Li Shang-yin

With the last one, we pass from the objective, physical world into a possible dream state in which time is cut off from its normal flux and becomes absolute in the sense that objects thus presented may become coextensive with one another. As usual, the visuality is remarkable. The unity here is one of shape and color, not causal relation of any kind.

Now a few complete poems of the authenticity of the perceiving act (I give here close approximations):

Dried vines, an old tree, evening crows;
A small bridge, flowing water, men's homes;
An ancient road, west winds, a lean horse;
Sun slants west:
A heart-torn man at sky's end.
—Ma Chih-yuan (ca. 1260–ca. 1341)

This poem operates pictorially rather than semantically. The successive shots do not constitute a linear development (such as *how this leads to that*). Rather the objects coexist, as in a painting, and yet the mobile point of view has made it possible to temporalize the spatial units. And witness this poem:

A thousand mountains—no bird's flight.
A million paths—no man's trace.
Single boat. Bamboo-leaved cape. An old man.
Fishing alone. Ice-river. Snow
—Liu Tsung-yuan (773–819)

We need little orientation to notice that the camera-eye from a bird's-eye view with which we can at once take possession of the totality of the scene on a cosmic scale as in all the Chinese landscape paintings—zooms in upon one single object, an old man in the midst of the vast frozen river surrounded by snow. Unlike the film which often focuses on events to be strung together with a story line, the cinematic movement here reproduces the activities of the perceiving act of an intense moment, the total consciousness of which is not completed until all the visual moments are presented simultaneously—again as in our perception of a classical Chinese painting. The spatial tensions here—the immeasurable cosmic coexisting with a speck of human existence—put us in the center of Phenomenon, allowing us to reach out to the circumference.

We mentioned earlier the fact that Chinese poets would not force the perspective of the ego upon Phenomenon. This is most obvious in Chinese landscape painting in which we either should say there is no perspective in it (the artist having become the objects in Phenomenon) or there are revolving perspectives, viewing totality from different angles simultaneously. This happens also in Chinese poetry. We have seen, in almost all the examples given above and in the last quoted poem in particular, how the viewer-reader is made to move into the total environment to experience the visual events from different spatial angles. More intriguing are the following lines from Wen Ting-yün (ninth century).

1. 1.	雞	cock (n.)	1. 2.	人	man (n.)
	聲	crow (n.)		跡	trace (n.)
	茅	straw (n.)		板	plank (n)
	店	inn (n)		橋	bridge (n.)
	月	moon (n.)		霜	frost (n.)

These are selected details, objects in their purest form, given to us at one instant to constitute an atmosphere, an environment. It is an environment in which we move about rather than viewing it from a fixed distant angle because we can never be certain as to where, in the background, we should put the cock, the moon, the bridge: Are we to visualize these as "(At) cockcrow, the moon (is seen above) the straw inn/footprints (are seen upon) the frost (covering) the plank bridge (?)." There are other ways of locating these details: The moon need not be "above" the inn; it could very well be just barely seen above the horizon. Without determining the definite spatial relationships of the objects, without allotting them fixed positions as viewed from chosen perspectives, as any translation of these lines into English would be tempted to do, we are liberated to see them from different perspectives. As a result, we are enabled to cross the limits of words into the realm of sculpture, toward the act of perceiving a piece of sculpture whose total existence depends on our viewing it from different angles as we move around it.

This sculptural quality is superbly approximated in Wang Wei's "Mount Chungnan":

The Chungnan ranges verge on the Capital
Mountain upon mountain to sea's brim.
(viewer on level ground looking from afar—Moment I)

White clouds—looking back—close up
(viewer coming out—Moment II)

Green mists—entering—become nothing
(viewer entering—Moment III)

Terrestrial divisions change at the middle peak
(viewer atop peak looking down—Moment IV)

Shade and light differ with every valley
(viewer on both sides of Mount simultaneously—Moment V)

To stay over in some stranger's house—
Across the water, call to ask a woodcutter
(viewer down on level ground—Moment VI)

In one of the volunteer sessions on the structure of the Chinese characters held in
an American grade school, after I had finished explaining how some of the Chinese
characters are pictorially based, how the signs match the actual objects, one boy
proceeded naively to pose a sagacious question: "All these are nouns, how are they
to form ideas?" It seems legitimate to pose the same question regarding many of the
Chinese lines above. I believe the question is answered, in part, in my earlier analy-
sis of a Liu Tsung-yüan poem, in which the spatial tensions and relationships be-
tween the immeasurable cosmic scene and a speck of human existence in the figure
of an old man fishing, project out, *without comment*, a meaning of the condition of
man in nature. All the other lines can be understood in a similar light.

Returning to the boy's question: I answered him by bringing out another cat-
egory of Chinese character structures. The two characters I chose were 時 and 言 .
The etymological origin of 時 (time) consists of the pictograph of ⊙ (sun) and 止 ,
the latter being a pictograph developed from an ancient picture of a foot touching
the ground 止 which came to mean both *stop* (the modern form of which is 止)
and *go* (the modern form of which is 之). Thus, the earliest Chinese viewed the
stop-and-go of the sun, the measured movement of the sun, as the idea "time." The
earliest pictographic stage of 言 was 言, denoting a mouth blowing a flute (the tip
of a Chinese flute). This character now means "speech," "expression," "message,"
which, to the people of the first harmony, was to be in rhythmic measure. Here, in
both cases, two visual objects juxtapose to form an idea. As we may now recall, this
structural principle of the Chinese character inspired Sergei Eisenstein to conceive
the technique of montage in the film.[14] The same structural principle continues to
be at work in Chinese poetry. One line from a Li Po poem which I discussed in great
detail in my book *Ezra Pound's Cathay* (Princeton, 1969) was:

浮 雲 遊 子 意
Floating cloud(s): wanderer's mood

Let me quote the relevant parts:

> Does the line mean, syntactically, "floating clouds *are* a wanderer's mood"...
> or "floating clouds *are like a* wanderer's mood"...? The answer is: it does and it
> does not at the same time. No one would fail to perceive the resemblance of a
> wanderer's drifting life ... to the floating clouds. But there is a flash of interest
> in the syntactically uncommitted resemblance which the introduction of "are"
> and "are like" destroys. In this case, we actually see the floating clouds and the
> wanderer (and the state of mind he is in) simultaneously. This simultaneous

14. Sergei Eisenstein, *Film Form and Film Sense,* trans. Jay Leyda (New York, 1942), chap. 3, "The Cin-
ematographic Principle and the Ideogram," p. 28.

presence of two objects, like the juxtaposition of two separate shots, resembles [in Eisenstein's words] "not so much a simple sum of one shot plus another shot—as it does a *creation*. It resembles a creation—rather than a sum of its parts—from the circumstance that in every such juxtaposition *the result is qualitatively* distinguishable from each component element viewed separately."[15]

Similarly, we have the following lines that by the sheer fact of montage using independent but juxtaposed visual events, point to an idea without allowing into the presentation the interference of the rhetoric of commentary. In the line,

國　破　山　　河　在
empire/broken/mountain/river/exist (remain)

The reader feels, *without being told,* the contrast and tension in the scenery so presented, and the introduction of explanatory elaboration will destroy the immediate contact between the viewer and the scene, as in the case of this typical translation and many others:

> *Though* a country be sundered, hills and rivers endure
> (italics mine)
> —Bynner[16]

Whether using montage or mobile points of view in the perceiving act, the Chinese poets give paramount importance to the acting-out of visual objects and events, letting them explain themselves by their coexisting, coextensive emergence from nature, letting the spatial tensions reflect conditions and situations rather than coercing these objects and events into some preconceived artificial orders by sheer human interpretive elaboration. In a line like Li Po's,

鳳去　　臺空　　江自流
Phoenix gone, terrace empty, river flows on alone
(shot 1)　　　(shot 2)　　　(shot 3)

do we need any more words to explain the vicissitude of time versus the permanence of Nature? Or in these lines from Tu Fu's "Autumn Meditation,"

Jade/dew/wither v./wound v./maple/tree/grove
Wu/mountain/Wu/gorges/air/grave—/desolate
river/middle/waves/—/embrace (include)/sky/surge v.
Pass/top/wind(s)/clouds/connect/ground/shadow(s)

15. *Ezra Pound's Cathay,* p. 22. Quote from Eisenstein, *Film Form and Film Sense,* p. 7.
16. Bynner, *The Jade Mountain,* p. 119.

[A. C. Graham's translation:

Gems of dew wilt and wound the maple trees in the wood:
From Wu mountains, from Wu gorges, the air blows desolate,
The waves between the river banks merge in the seething sky,
Clouds in the wind above the passes touch their shadows on the ground.
—*Poems of the Late T'ang* (Penguin, 1962), p. 52]

where the curves of the external climate coincide with the curves of the internal climate of the aging poet, do we need to falsify their identity by turning them into puppets of some Grand Idea?

PART II

The success of the Chinese poets in authenticating the fluctuation of concrete events in Phenomenon, their ability to preserve the multiple relationships in a kind of penumbra of indeterminateness, depends to a great extent upon the sparseness of syntactical demands. This helps the poet to highlight independent visual events, leaving them in coextensive spatial relationships. And this language, as a medium for poetry, would not have become what it is without the support of a unique aesthetic horizon—easy loss of self into the undifferentiated mode of existence—ordained by centuries of art and poetry. There is an inseparability between medium and poetics, between language and world view. The question now arises: how can a language of rigid syntactical rules, such as English, approximate successfully the mode of presentation whose success depends upon freedom from syntax? The reverse question is also imminent: how can an epistemological world view developed from the Platonic and Aristotelian metaphysics, which emphasize the ego in search of knowledge of the non-ego, having taken up the task of classifying *being* in concepts, propositions, and ordered structures, turn around and endorse a medium that belies the function and process of epistemological elaboration? The answer is: impossible, if the Platonic dichotomy of the phenomenal and the noumenal (appearance and reality) and the Aristotelian "universal logical structures" persist without any sort of adjustment. If one attempted to turn the English language into one of broken, unsyntactical units and demanded that it become a medium for poetry, he would be excommunicated rather than anointed so long as no attempt has been made to widen the possibilities of the Western aesthetic horizon to include the *other* perspectivism, at least to exist coextensively with the native world view. It is at this juncture that the discussion of convergence becomes most cogent and significant.

16

The adjustment of Western world views in modern times is a book in itself. No such attempt is to be made here. Without going into the complicated history of this adjustment, it is sufficient to say one thing—namely, all modern thought and art, from the phenomenologists to as late as Jean Dubuffet's *Anticultural Positions,* began with a rejection of abstract systems (particularly those of Plato and Aristotle) in order to return to concrete existence. Almost all the phenomenologists posed this question, and Heidegger's request to return to the *appeal* of beings gathered momentum in many later philosophers and artists. Meanwhile, Bergson, who was in essence still an epistemological philosopher, pointed a way toward the "liquidation of the romantic self." The philosophical rationalization of the subject has been closely examined by Wylie Sypher in his book *Loss of the Self in Modern Literature and Art* (New York, 1962, 1964). For our purpose we will focus on a few statements by Anglo-American critics and poets at the turn of the century which have led to a subtle adjustment of the poetic language to the degree that it literally violates traditional syntactical structures. My central interest in this part is with some of the potentials of this process of change in the English language.

Direct entry into the matter, then:

> Not the fruit of experience, but experience itself, is the end . . . to burn always with this hard, gem-like flame.[17]
> [Ancient thought sought] to arrest every object in an eternal outline. . . .
> [the modern spirit asserts that] nothing is or can be rightly known except relatively and under conditions . . . [modern man becomes] so receptive, all the influences of nature and of society ceaselessly playing upon him, so that every hour in his life is unique, changed altogether by a stray word, or glance, or touch. It is the truth of these relations that experience gives us, not the truth of eternal outlines ascertained once for all, but a world of gradations. . . .[18]

"Experience itself" is the key; "a world of gradations" not "the eternal outlines ascertained once for all" of the Platonic ideas. Echoing Pater but developed from Bergson, T. E. Hulme:

> The ancients were perfectly aware of the fluidity of the world and of its impermanence . . . but while they recognized it, they feared it and endeavoured to evade it, to construct things of permanence which would stand fast in this universal flux which frightened them. They had the disease, the passion, for immortality. They wished to construct things which should be proud boasts that they, men, were immortal. We see it in a thousand different forms. Materially in the pyramids, spiritually in the dogmas of religion and in the hypostatized ideas of Plato.[19]

17. Pater, *The Renaissance* (London, 1922), pp. 236–237.
18. Pater, *Appreciations* (London, 1924), pp. 66–68.
19. T. E. Hulme, *Further Speculations,* ed. Sam Hynes (Lincoln, Neb., 1955), pp. 70–71.

Instead of hypostatized ideas and constructions of the arrogant self, Hulme asks that poetry be

> not a counter language, but a visual concrete one. It is a compromise for a language of intuition which would hand over sensations bodily. It always endeavours to arrest you, and to make you continually see a physical thing, to prevent you from gliding through an abstract process.[20]

and one of the methods to achieve this is:

> Say the poet is moved by a certain landscape, he selects from that certain images which, put into juxtaposition in separate lines, serve to suggest and to evoke the state he feels.... Two visual images form what one may call a visual chord. They unite to suggest an image which is different to both.[21]

This is montage: juxtaposition of two visual events to create a third that is different from both. The method is, to Hulme, an alternative to the process of explanation in which syntax plays an important role. Syntax unfolds the intensive manifold, the vital reality, into an extensive manifold, a mechanical complexity.[22]

In 1911, before Pound came into contact with Chinese poetry, he argued:

> The artist seeks out the luminous detail and presents it. He does not comment.[23]

After Pound's contact with Chinese poetry:

> It is because certain Chinese poets have been content to set forth their matter without moralizing and without comment that one labors to make a translation.[24]

Early in 1901 Pound advised William Carlos Williams in similar terms, and later (1916) wrote to Iris Barry emphatically:

> ... The necessity for creating or constructing something; of presenting an image, or enough images of concrete things arranged to stir the reader ... I think there must be more, predominantly more, objects than statements and conclusions, which latter are purely optional, not essential, often superfluous and therefore bad.[25]

---

20. Hulme, *Speculations*, p. 134.

21. Hulme, *Further Speculations*, "A Lecture on Modern Poetry," p. 73.

22. More specifically, "Explanation means *ex plane,* that is to say, the opening out of things on a plain surface ... the process of explanation is always a process of unfolding. A tangled mass is unfolded flat so that you can see all its parts separated out, and any tangle which can be separated out in this way must of course be an extensive manifold," p. 177.

23. Ezra Pound, "I Gather the Limbs of Osiris," *New Age,* x.6 (December 7, 1911), p. 130.

24. Pound, "Chinese Poetry," *Today,* III (April 1918), p. 54.

25. Pound, *The Letters of Ezra Pound,* ed., D. D. Paige (New York, 1950), pp. 90-91.

Pound was practicing a form of montage at the end of an early poem "Cino"[26]—without, I am sure, being fully aware of its permanence in his poetry. His contact with the Japanese haiku and Chinese poetry and Chinese characters turned the technique into a central one in the *Cantos,* beginning with the famous "Metro" poem, through the juxtaposition of cultural moments as "luminous details," to the use of the Chinese ideogram as an amassing vortex.

Williams in his turn:

No ideas but in things[27]

He went further: "A life that is here and now is timeless . . . a new world that is always 'real' . . ."[28] and "no symbolism is acceptable,"[29] a true beginning to break away from the Platonic system to become, in Kenneth Burke's words, a poet of contact.[30] And Williams wants to see:

The thing itself without forethought or afterthought but
with great intensity of perception.[31]

And Olson and Creeley, in step with Pound and Williams:

The objects which occur at any given moment of composition . . . are, can be, must be treated exactly as they do occur therein and not by any ideas or preconceptions from outside the poem . . . must be handled as a series of objects in field . . . a series of tensions . . . space-tensions of a poem . . . the acting-on-you of the poem.[32]

But Hulme was arguing for a poetic ideal in front of which the English language, with all its rigid syntax for elaboration and clarification, becomes helpless. Hulme called for the destruction of syntax to achieve the concrete. The earliest attempt was made by Mallarmé. In order to arrive at a pure state of poetry of essences, to freely transpose objects and words for his construction of a world so absolute that it has no strings attached to physical reality, he dislocates syntax and, in his later sonnets, withdraws all the links that originally riveted the poem together.[33]

26. This part runs:
    I will sing of the white birds
    In the blue waters of heaven,
    The clouds that are spray to its sea.
27. William Carlos Williams, *Paterson* (New Directions, 1946, 1963), pt. 1, p. 6.
28. Williams, *Selected Essays* (New Directions, 1954, 1969), p. 196.
29. *Ibid.,* p. 213.
30. In Kenneth Burke, "Heaven's First Law," *Dial,* LXXI (1922), 197–200.
31. Williams, *Selected Essays,* p. 5.
32. Olson and Creeley, "Projective Verse," *Poetry New York,* no. 3 (1950), more conveniently now in Charles Olson's *Selected Writings* (New Directions, 1966), p. 20.
33. See Symon's "Mallarmé" in *The Symbolist Movement in Literature,* pp. 197–198; Frank Kermode, chapter on Symons in *The Romantic Image;* and my *Ezra Pound's Cathay,* pp. 48ff.

This absolutism of art, as well as his syntactical innovation, prepares the way for Pound to realize the poetic ideal that both Hulme and Pound, each in his own way, postulates. The adjustment of conventional English made by Pound to approximate the curves of experience has been a steady one. Compare (a) with (b)—(a) being the rearrangement of (b), Pound's "The Coming of War: Actaeon"—back to the traditional line format.

> (a) An image of Lethe, and the fields
> Full of faint light, but golden gray cliffs,
> And beneath them, a sea, harsher than granite . . .

> (b) An image of Lethe,
>   and the fields
> Full of faint light
>   but golden
> Gray cliffs,
>   and beneath them
> A sea
> Harsher than granite . . . .

The breakup of lines into small units graphically arranged serves to (1) promote the visuality of the images, (2) isolate them as independent visual events, (3) force the reader-viewer to perceive the poem in spatial counterpoints, (4) enhance the physicality of objects (such as "sea" literally and visually beneath the "Gray cliffs" that appear protruding out from above), and (5) activate the poem through phases of perception similar to the spotlighting effect or the mobile point of view. These effects, modified and refined, dominate the entire *Cantos*. In this instance, Pound uses a space break to occasion a time break; he has not yet dealt actively with syntactical break. The latter aspect started with the "Metro" poem and the whole discussion of the superpository technique by Pound now too famous to need repetition here, launched him into the more daring innovation of the medium. The poem was modeled after the Japanese *haiku* and he examined an example in his essay "Vorticism" (1914):

> The footsteps of the cat upon the snow:
> (are like) plum blossoms.

Pound explained: "The words 'are like' would not occur in the original."[34] And Pound did precisely that in his "Metro" poem:

> The apparition of these faces in the crowd;
> Petals on a wet, black bough.

Taking away the word "like" disrupts the syntax, giving prominence and independence to the two visual events, letting them coexist, one interdefining the other.

34. Pound, *Fortnightly Review,* XCVI (Sept. 1, 1914), 471. Reprinted in Pound's *Gaudier-Brzeska,* pp. 94–109.

The early version of it published in *Poetry* of 1913 brings out Pound's obsession with visual order and the importance of the perceiving act. It runs:

The apparition	of these faces	in the crowd:
Petals	on a wet, black	bough.

Here we find space break and syntactical break, both of which are employed in the *Cantos*. This graphic innovation is first found in his translation of *Cathay*.

> Surprised. Desert turmoil. Sea sun.
> —"South-Folk in Cold Country"

which Pound mistranslated from the crippled Fenollosa notes, a fact that I discussed in full in my book *Ezra Pound's Cathay*.[35] Here what we are interested in is the resemblance of this line, syntactically speaking, to some of the Chinese lines we have seen. Space break, syntactical break, superimposition of one impression of bewilderment and disorder upon another; and the images are of synchronous relations. More is to come in the *Cantos* which I will simply outline without comment:

(a) Rain; empty river, a voyage
     . . . .
     Autumn moon; hills rise above lakes
     . . . .
     Broad water; geese line out with the autumn.   49/38

(b) Prayer: hands uplifted
     Solitude: a person, a Nurse   54/101

(c) Moon,   cloud,   tower,   a patch of the battistero
     all of whiteness   79/62

I would like to add here that example (a) is from Canto 49, which is constructed out of a series of Chinese poems (i.e., in Chinese) written by a Japanese on an album of paintings modeled after the Chinese art-motif of "Eight Views of Hsiao-hsiang." In that poem, Pound, using a crib (which I have seen)[36] done by a Chinese in Italy, keeps the closest to the Chinese syntax. One may perhaps say that with this poem, Pound finally ordains his innovation, not only for himself but for many others to come, including Gary Snyder.

Similar to Pound's graphic and syntactical innovation is that done by his close friend William Carlos Williams, who was partially influenced by Pound and to a greater degree inspired by the "Armory Show" of 1913. This presentation of avant-garde paintings, including Marcel Duchamp's famous *Nude Descending a Staircase*, has been carefully treated by Professor Dijkstra in his *The Hieroglyphics of a New Speech* (Princeton, 1969). We will find that much of what we learned from some of

---

35. See particularly the part subtitled "Graphic Ironical Play" for full treatment of this technique, pp. 143 ff. Discussion of the line in question is on pp. 125–128.
36. Courtesy of Hugh Kenner.

the Chinese lines and from Pound's graphic innovation can be applied to Williams. Compare:

(a) So much depends upon a red wheelbarrow
     glazed with rain water beside the white chickens.

(b) so much depends
     upon

     a red wheel
     barrow

     glazed with rain
     water

     beside the white
     chickens.

(a) being a rearrangement of Williams's poem (b) into conventional line-structure. We can see easily here how the space break enhances the visuality of the different phases of the perception of an object, how words gain independence and liberation from the linearity of the normal line-structures and how these independent visual events or moments bring about the changing perspectives of one object. As a result, the reader-viewer is transposed into the midst of the scene reaching out spatially to the different visual phases of this object.

These are also true of "Nantucket":

Flowers through the window
lavender and yellow

Changed by white curtains—
Smell of cleanliness

Sunshine of late afternoon
On the glass tray

A glass pitcher, the tumbler
turned down, by which

a key is tying—and the
immaculate white bed

This technique of space break coupled with syntactical break (there are many incomplete sentences in Williams) forces the reader to focus attention, at *all times,* (*this is the lesson that Olson and Creeley learned*), upon the urgency of every moment as it occurs in the process of the perceiving act. Williams happily approved the essay "Projective Verse" by Olson (and Creeley) as an extension and clarification of his technique. The following passage can indeed be considered a footnote to the perceiving process of Williams:

ONE PERCEPTION MUST IMMEDIATELY AND DIRECTLY LEAD TO A FURTHER PERCEPTION. It means exactly what it says, is a matter of, at *all* points . . . get on with it, keep moving, keep in, speed, the nerves, their speed, the perceptions, theirs, the acts, the split second acts, the whole business, keep it moving as fast as you can, citizen. And if you also set up as a poet, USE USE USE the process at all points, in any given poem always, always one perception must must must MOVE, INSTANTER, ON ANOTHER![37]

Williams's attempt at syntactical break can be best seen in the poem "The Locust Tree in Flower." A comparison between the early and later versions will sharpen for us the issue in question:

Early version (Poetry, 1933)	Later version
Among	Among
the leaves	of
bright	green
green	stiff
of wrist-thick	old
tree	bright
and old	broken
stiff broken	branch
branch	come
ferncool	white
swaying	sweet
loosely	May
come May	again
again	
white blossom	
clusters	
hide	
to spill	
their sweets	
almost	
unnoticed	
down	
and quickly	
fall	

37. Olson, *Selected Writings*, p. 17.

The early version, like many of his other poems, by dint of the space break, accentuates the different phases of the perceiving act. But, like them too, there is a continuity in syntax ("Nantucket" excepted). The revised version is something else. First of all, "Among," among what? "Of," of what? These prepositions have literally become *position* words, to put us in the position of being in the midst of something, then to change perspective and spatial relationship *Of;* to change perspective again to notice sheer *green* (color so strong that it takes full possession of the viewer); and then *old,* etc. In other words, we notice the qualities and the growth and change of these qualities which mime the flowering process of the locust tree. Language of gestures: fricatives (*"bright," "broken," "branch"*) reflecting the inner struggle of growth until *"come,"* with open vowel operating. This poem matches Zaslove's description of how gestures and movements have to reflect the life-mechanism of the moment in order to authenticate it. In this poem, too, like the flexibility of the Chinese syntax, the usual allotment of grammatical function to each word is erased. Indeed, to view this poem from a normal understanding of English grammar, one is bound to say: No, it is not English at all; it does not fulfill the requirement of a language. But, supported by the poetic power of communication that the poem has, ordained by its own laws of energy distribution that reflect the activities of the perceiving moment, these words survive as an adequate medium.

Creeley is perhaps the very first person who fully understands this miming of energy-discharge, to use his term. He says

> If one thinks of the literal root of the word *verse,* "a line, furrow, turning- *vertere,* to turn . . . ," he will come to a sense of "free verse" as that instance of writing in poetry which "turns" upon an occasion intimate with, in fact, the issue of, its own nature rather than to an abstract decision of "form" taken from a prior instance. The point is, simply enough, why does the "line" thus "turn" and what does inform it in that movement?[38]

Yes, Creeley, unlike Williams, is a subjective poet who writes about intimate moments he once "stumbled into": "warmth for a night perhaps, the misdirected intention came right . . . a sudden instance of love."[39] And as such, he very seldom emphasizes the visual events as does Williams, but the same obsession with promoting the physical presence of an experience (even though a subjective one) has driven Creeley to employ, in his poems, I think, to his advantage, the kind of space breaks and syntactical breaks ordained by Pound and Williams and, we must not forget, by E. E. Cummings, whose graphic arrangement of language into gestures to reflect the ritualistic procedures of a moment (as in "In-Just") makes him one of the forerunners of the now famous concrete poetry. Creeley's "La Noche," for instance,

---

38. Statement on "Open Form," in *Naked Poetry,* ed. Stephen Berg and Robert Mezey (New York, 1969).
39. Preface to *For Love.*

La Noche

In the court-
yard at midnight, at

midnight. The moon is
locked in itself, to

a man a
familiar thing

would not work if recast back to a normal line-structure. The repetition (in nor-
mal line-structure) of "at midnight" will become rhetorical and superfluous,
but graphically separated, leaving "midnight" and "the moon" in the center of the
poem, "locked in" as it were, within the arms of the poet's awareness, we can feel the
"turning" (physically felt) from the outside daily world into the inner familiar mo-
ment in which the poet finds himself.

I will conclude this part with poems of Gary Snyder, who has inherited Han Shan
and Wang Wei (at present he is working on Tu Fu and reading Hsieh Ling-Yün)[40]
on the one hand and has incorporated the Pound-Williams sense of language on
the other:

1. Burning the small dead
            branches
        broke from beneath
        Thick spreading white pine.
                    a hundred summers
    snowmelt   rock   and air

        hiss in a twisted bough

                sierra granite;

            ιιιt Ritter
                black rock twice as old

    Deneb, Altair

    Windy fire.
    —"Burning the Small Dead"

40. Gary Snyder's affinity with Han Shan began with his own way of living. He was in isolation on the
High Sierras for five months and when he came back to the Bay Area, he was reading Han Shan at the
University of California, Berkeley. He told me that the images in the Han Shan poems (in the original)
were practically his. As for his interest in the other poets, one can detect this easily in his nature poems.
He told me that Wang Wei was one of his first poets and he continues: "I am more Chinese in tempera-
ment."

2. Well water
   cool in
   Summer
   warm in
   winter
   . . . .
   —"Eight Sandbars on the Takano River"

3. First day of the world
   white rock ridges
                     new born
   Jay chatters   the first time
   Rolling a smoke by the campfire
   New! never before.
                     bitter coffee, cold
   Dawn wind, sun on the cliffs,
   . . . .
   —"Hunting" No. 15

This introduction is exploratory: it looks toward, rather than ending up in, an ideal convergence between two languages and two poetics, toward an awareness that can perhaps lead to an actual cultural convergence when and if our readers would take it seriously one day to adjust and attune their life-style, world view and art-style according to the new intellectual horizon.

POSTSCRIPT

Wordsworth once argued: "Minds that have nothing to confer / Find little to perceive." We would accept this conception of the interworkings between mind and nature, if it allows a "conferring" of significance without the large paragraphs of exploratory thinking moving through a process of intellection, turning observations into arguments. In one sense, Wordsworth has belied his Nature, in which no intellect is supposed to be at work, and his lesson of "wise passiveness," by a conscious conferring of heuristic significance through syllogistic progression. This manner of conferring is, of course, central to much of Western poetry. With Wordsworth, as with Kant, pure perception of phenomena is not sufficient; an epistemological synthesis must be achieved by "the conferring, the abstracting and the modifying powers of imagination."

We must admit, however, that in Chinese poetry, insofar as it is written in language, there is necessarily an act of conferring in the poet's perception. But the Chinese alternative, as outlined in the foregoing pages, offers something *signifi-*

cantly different from the syllogistic procedures of Western poetry. Both the Taoist and the Confucian poetics demand the submission of the self to the cosmic measure rather than the Kantian attempt to resist and measure oneself against the apparent almightiness of nature, resulting in a much greater degree of noninterference in artistic presentation. Even the poets bent on the didactic side of the Confucian poetics employ this presentation to balance off the possible dilution into pure philosophical abstraction.

It is these significant differences that we want to highlight, hoping to put the readers out of gear, so to speak, so that they can more enjoy the specific aesthetic horizon of the Chinese. Furthermore, the implications of this alternative will also help the modern Anglo-American poetics to find anchor in their search for a new aesthetic ground. As such, this introduction has not covered the whole spectrum of variations of critical theories in China, nor does it contain a full account of the historical changes in the rhetoric of the Chinese poetics. The special mode of apprehension and presentation in Chinese poetry, like any aesthetic attitude, is not born overnight; it takes years of modification to arrive at maturity as a cult. The anthology that follows, arranged in chronological order and according to modes and genres, is intended to help the readers trace the morphology of such an attitude, the full expression of which is to be found in the poetry of T'ang Dynasty.

FROM THE *SHIH CHING* OR

THE *BOOK OF SONGS*

Shih Ching (*The Classic of Poetry*) or *The Book of Songs* (compiled sometime after 600 B.C.) represents the earliest specimens of ancient Chinese poetry. Confucius is supposed to have made this selection of 300-odd pieces from an original collection of 3,000. Most of these songs are communal in origin, connected with courtship, marriage, and ceremonial activities in seasonal festivals (nos. 1, 23, 95 in the present selection) and retain much of the formulaic character of oral poetry: From line to stanza, from stanza to stanzas; elementary procedures of reduplications, repetitions, variations, and symmetry; within the poem, ready-made phrases, borrowed lines and even stanzas, stock images, and situations; thematically, in place of individualistic sentiments, communal events presented in an impersonal manner showing little or no soul-cry of the ego, no deliberate, premeditated threads of development. And yet, when compared to other specimens of primitive poetry, such as those by the Semang (see Bowra, *Primitive Song*, p. 66), these songs display a greater degree of artistic manipulation: they are more formalized and there are more sophisticated stanzaic divisions and contrapuntal correspondence to keep pace with music and dance movements (which are now lost). These traces of workmanship affirm the fact that they have been retouched, sometimes with meticulous care, by poet-musicians.

In his *Analects,* Confucius assigned a utilitarian and didactic function to the *Book of Songs:*

> For the Songs will help you to incite people's emotions, to observe their feelings, to keep company, to express your grievances. They may be used at home in the service of one's father; abroad, in the service of one's prince. Moreover, they will widen your acquaintance with the names of birds, beasts, plants and trees. [XVII.9]

> If out of the three hundred *Songs,* I had to take one phrase to cover all my teaching, I would say, "Let there be no evil in your thoughts." [II.2; translation by Waley]

This view, much expanded and exploited by later statesmen-Confucianists, had deviated into an imposing amount of moralistic interpretations that greatly distorted the very natural and naive beauty of these rustic love songs. Song No. 23 (see text), for instance, which is an animated pastiche of a lovely rustic seducement song, is encumbered with the following didactic purposefulness. Let me quote Marcel Granet's translation of the orthodox notes to this poem in full:

Preface: *The Dead Doe* (shows) abhorrence of the failure to observe the rites. The kingdom was in a state of great disorder (at the end of the Yin dynasty). Ruffianism prevailed and manners became demoralized. When the civilizing influence of King Wen made itself felt although the period was still one of disorder, yet the absence of rites was deplored.

Failure to observe the rites: no intermediary employed and no ceremonial presents sent (wild geese and lengths of silk), marriages consummated by force. (Cheng.)

In times of distress ceremonial presents decreased in value. (Instead of the deer-skin which should have been sent), (*I li,* Marriage), the girl hopes that some of the flesh of a deer that has been killed and divided by the hunters may be sent to her wrapped in couch-grass. (Mao and Cheng.) (*Chou li,* Biot, i, 208.) Presents of food must be presented on a bed of herbs. (*Li chi, Chueh li,* Couvreur, i. 45.) The couch-grass, being white, was used because of its purity. (Mao.) Cf. *I ching.*

3 and 4. The young girl thinks longingly of the spring because it is not lawful for her to await the autumn. (Mao.) Mao thinks that the girl had reached 20, the limit of the marriage age. She cannot wait for the autumn-winter season (according to Mao, the proper marriage season), but thinks longingly of the spring, the time when marriages could take place summarily, in which rites and ceremonial presents are not essential.

Cheng is of opinion that the second month of spring was the recognized time for the completion of marriages. The girl thinks of the time when, in accordance with the rites, it will be permissible for her to unite with the boy. It was necessary for the boy first of all to send an intermediary to ask for her hand (line 4). Cheng believes that the preliminary betrothal ceremonies took place in autumn. Cf. L. 1 and 2.

5 and 6. A bundle of firewood wrapped in white reeds like the deer-flesh, also served as a ceremonial present [again the theory of the decreased value of the ritual gifts during times of disorder (Cheng.)]

8. Virtue like jade. Owing to its whiteness and its strength jade is symbolic of the girl's virtue.

9. A descriptive auxiliary is here used to depict an attitude in which there is no violence.

10. A sash attached to the girdle. (Mao.) This sash is an important item of feminine dress. On the birth of a girl such a sash was hung at the door. *Li chi, Wei tse,* Couvreur, i, 663. When the girl set out on the wedding journey (*Shih ching,* Pin feng, 4; Couvreur, 167), her mother fastened a sash to her girdle when she gave her parting instructions (*I li,* Marriage note). On the marriage night the matron in charge of the girl presented it to her after she had undressed

(*I li* Marriage). She used it to cleanse herself (Cheng, note on *I li* Marriage). To touch the sash denotes the consummation of the marriage.

11. More particularly a large hound in the grass. (Mao.) The dogs bark when violence is offered to anyone in defiance of the rites. (Mao.) Marcel Granet, p. 118–119 (see Bibliography).

The deification of Confucius since the Han Dynasty had made the *Book of Songs* a must for every scholar-poet in the imperial examination through which statesmanship was to be achieved. It had also left these interpretations unchallenged for more than sixteen centuries to come. This formidable phenomenon had, in turn, created a double life or identity for the *Book of Songs.* Both the original imaginative process of arresting the essential, vivid and immediate details of an experience and the later Confucian interpretations imposed upon these poems went into the creative consciousness of the scholar-poets—a curious sort of cultural transformation.

關雎

關關雎鳩　在河之洲　窈窕淑女　君子好逑
參差荇菜　左右流之　窈窕淑女　寤寐求之
求之不得　寤寐思服　悠哉悠哉　輾轉反側
參差荇菜　左右采之　窈窕淑女　琴瑟友之
參差荇菜　左右芼之　窈窕淑女　鐘鼓樂之

34

NO. I. *KUAN-KUAN, THE OSPREYS*

1.	*Kuan -* (onomatopoeic)	*Kuan*	osprey/s	
2.	on; in; at	river	's	isle
3.	delicate; lovely; slender		nice; good	girl
4.	gentleman/'s		fit; good	mate
5.	of-different-lengths; long-and-short		duckweed/s	
6.	left	right	flow (get)	(it)
7.	delicate; lovely; slender		nice; good	girl
8.	wake	sleep	seek	(her)
9.	seek	(her)	not	get
10.	wake	sleep	think	(-of-her)
11.	long; distant; deep	O!	long; distant; deep	O!
12.	toss	turn	turn-to	side
13.	of-different-lengths; long-and-short		duckweed/s	
14.	lute	right	pluck	(it)
15.	delicate; lovely;		nice; good	girl
16.	lute	zither	(be) friend	(her)
17.	of-different-length long-and-short		duckweed/s	
18.	left	right	choose	(it)
19.	delicate; lovely; slender		nice; good	girl
20.	bell/s	drum/s	please (welcome)	(her)

1.	*Kuan-kuan,* the ospreys.	11.	So distant, so deep;
2.	On the river's isle.	12	Toss and turn in bed.
3.	Delicate, a good girl:	13.	Long and short, duckweeds.
4.	A gentleman's fit mate.	14.	Pluck some—left and right.
5.	Long and short, duckweeds.	15.	Delicate, a good girl:
6.	Fetch some—left and right.	16.	With music to befriend her.
7.	Delicate, a good girl.	17.	Long and short, duckweeds.
8.	Waking, sleeping: seek her.	18.	Pick some—left and right.
9.	To seek her and possess not—	19.	Delicate, a good girl:
10.	Waking, sleeping: think of her.	20.	With bells and drums to meet her.

麕

野有死麕，白茅包之。有女懷春，吉士誘之。
林有樸樕，野有死鹿。白茅純束，有女如玉。
舒而脫脫兮，無感我帨兮，無使尨也吠。

NO. 23. IN THE WILDS, A DEAD DOE

1.	wild/s	there-is	dead	deer (hornless-river=deer)	
2.	white	grass; reed/s	wrap	(it)	
3.	there-is	girl	cherish	spring (-feeling, i.e., at age of puberty)	
4.	fine; handsome	gentleman	entice; solicit	(her)	
5.	woods	there-is are	small-bush/es		
6.	wilds	there-is	dead	deer	
7.	white	grass; reed/s	bind	bundle (v.)	
8.	there-is	girl	like	jade	
9.	slow	(particle)	slow	slow take-it-easy	(caesura-apostrophe)
10.	do-not	move	my	kerchief; sash	(caesura-apostrophe)
11.	do-not	make	dog	(part.)	bark

1. In the wilds, a dead doe.
2. White reeds to wrap it.
3. A girl, spring-touched:
4. A fine man to seduce her.
5. In the woods, bushes.
6. In the wilds, a dead deer.
7. White reeds in bundles.
8. A girl like jade.
9. Slowly. Take it easy.
10. Don't feel my sash!
11. Don't make the dog bark!

離　黍

離離苗靡搖者　　　　　　　憂　何　求
離之靡搖者我蒼人　　　謂　心　我　謂
黍稷遯心我知悠何黍　　　我　　謂
彼黍行中知不悠此彼
彼彼行中知不悠此彼

離離穗靡醉者　　　　　　　憂　何　求
離之靡如者我蒼人　　　謂　心　我　謂
黍稷遯心我知悠何黍　　　我　　謂
彼黍行中知不悠此彼
彼彼行中知不悠此彼稷

1.	that those	millet/s
2.	that those	sorghum
3.	walk going	long-way
4.	mid-central	heart
5.	know (i.e., those who know me)	me
6.	not	know
7.	distant	distant
8.	this	what-kind-of what-sort-of
9.	that those	millet/s
10.	that those	sorghum
11.	walk going	long-way
12.	mid central	heart
13.	know	me
14.	not	know
15.	distant	distant
16.	this	what-kind-of what-sort-of
17.	that those	millet/s
18.	that those	sorghum

drooping-full	drooping-full				
's	sprout/s				
slowly	slowly				
shaken	shaken				
tossed	tossed				
(those)		say	my I	heart	sad distressed grieved
me	(those)	say	I	what	desire be up to be after
blue	Heaven				
man	O				
drooping-full	drooping-full				
's	ears				
slowly	slowly				
like	drunk intoxicated				
(those)		say	my I	heart	sad distressed grieved
me	(those)	say	I	what	desire be-up-to
blue	Heaven				
man	O				
drooping-full	drooping-full				
's	grain/s				

行邁靡靡　　　謂我心憂
中心如噎　　　謂我何求
知我者　　　　悠悠蒼天
不知我者　　　此何人哉
悠悠
此

40

slowly	slowly				
like	choked blocked				
(those)		say	my I	heart	sad distressed grieved
me	(those)	say	I	what	desire be-up-to be-after
blue	Heaven				
man	O				

1. Millets in full rows
2. Sorghum in sprouts
3. Long walk so slow
4. A heart all tossed
5. Those who know me say: He is distressed.
6. Those who do not know me say: What is he up to?
7. Under this easy, wide blue
8. What sort of man is he?
9. Millets in full rows
10. Sorghum in spikes
11. Long walk so slow
12. A heart all drunk
13. Those who know me say: He is distressed.
14. Those who do not know me say: What is he up to?
15. Under this easy, wide blue
16. What sort of man is he?
17. Millets in full rows
18. Sorghums in grains
19. Long walk so slow
20. A heart all blocked
21. Those who know me say: He is distressed.
22. Those who do not know me say: What is he up to?
23. Under this easy, wide blue
24. What sort of man is he?

溱 洧

溱與洧，方渙渙兮。
士與女，方秉蕑兮。
女曰觀乎？士曰既且。
且往觀乎？洧之外，
洵訏且樂。
維士與女，伊其相謔，
贈之以勺藥。

溱與洧，瀏其清矣。
士與女，殷其盈矣。
女曰觀乎？士曰既且。
且往觀乎？洧之外，
洵訏且樂。
維士與女，伊其將謔，
贈之以勺藥。

1. Chen   and
    (i.e., the two rivers)
2. boys   and
    gentlemen
3. girl   say
4. boy   say
5. again   go
    why-not
    but
6. Wei   's
    (i.e., beyond
    the Wei)
7. (therefore)   boy
    (thus)
    (upon this)
8. (part.)   (them)

9. present-as-gift   (him, her)
10. Chen   and

11. boy   and

12. girl   say

13. boy   say
14. why-not   go
    again
15. Chen   's

16. (therefore)   boy
    (thus)
    (upon-this)

17. (part.)   (them)

18. present-as-gift   (him, her)

Wei		now	brimming	brimming	(caes.-apos.)
	at-the-point-of				
girls		now	hold	orchids	(caes.-apos.)
ladies			pick		
see	(interro.-exclam.)				
already	(part.)				
see	(interro.-exclam.)				
view					
beyond		really	large	and	fun
			spacious	in-addition-to	pleasant
and	girl				
mutual	dally				
with-each-	sport				
other	have-fun				
	make-merry				
with	peony				
Wei		deep	(part.)	clear	(part.-
		clear			exclam.)
girl		crowd	(they)	fill	(part.-
		multitudinous		full	-exclam.)
see	(interro.-exclam.)				
view					
already	(part.)				
see	(interro. exclam.)				
view					
beyond		really	large	and	fun
			spacious	in-addition-to	pleasant
and	girl				
shall	make-merry, etc.				
mutual					
with-each-other					
with	peony				

1. The Chen and Wei are brimming.
2. Boys and girls go orchid-picking.
3. Let's go and see, she says.
4. I already did, answers he.
5. So what, go again,
6. Beyond the Wei is fun, a full plain.
7. Men and women
8. Make merry
9. And give each other a peony.
10. The Chen and Wei runs clear.
11. Boys and girls, a blooming spree.
12. Let's go and see, she says.
13. I already did, answers he.
14. So what, go again,
15. Beyond the Wei is fun, a full plain.
16. Men and women
17. Make merry
18. And give each other a peony.

采薇

薇止歸止家故居故薇止歸止烈渴定聘薇

采薇采作日莫靡之啟之采柔日憂烈載未歸采

薇亦歸亦室玁遑玁薇亦歸亦心飢戍使薇曰

日歲靡玁不玁采薇曰心憂載我靡采

NO. 167. PICK FERNS, PICK FERNS

1. pick	fern	pick	fern
2. fern	(part.)	sprout	(part.)
3. (part.)	return	(part.)	return
4. year	(part.)	dusk (v.)	(part.)
5. no	house	no	home
6. Hsien	Yün	's	cause

(i.e., because of Hsien-yün, barbarians from the North)

7. no	time	kneel	sit
		(i.e., rest)	
8. Hsien	Yün	's	cause
9. pick	fern	pick	fern
10. fern	(part.)	tender	(part.)
11. (part.)	return	(part.)	return
12. heart	(part.)	worry	(part.)
13. worried	heart	burn	burn
14. (part.)	hungry	(part.)	thirsty
15. I	guard	not-yet	settle
My	garrison		at-an-end
Our			
16. no	messenger	return	inquire
17. pick	fern	pick	fern

45

止歸止臨處疾來何華何車駕業居揭牡騤騤依腓翼

剛曰陽靡啓孔不維之斯之毗業定三四騤所所翼

亦歸亦事遑心行爾常路子車牡敢月彼牡子人牡

薇曰歲王不憂我彼維彼君戎四豈一駕四君小四

18.	fern	(part.)	stiff	(part.)
			coarse	
19.	(part.)	return	(part.)	return
20.	year	(part.)	tenth-month	(part.)
21.	emperor's	affair	no	rest
22.	no	time	kneel	sit
23.	worried	heart	quite	distressed
				sick
24.	I	go	not	come
25.	That	blooming	(part.)	what
26.	(part.)	cherry	's	flower
27.	that	chariot	(part.)	what
				whose
28.	emperor	—	's	chariot
29.	war	chariot	already	yoked
	martial			
30.	four	horses	strong	—
31.	how	dare	settle	rest
32.	one	month	three	battles
33.	drive	those	four	horses
34.	four	horses	strong	—
35.	gentlemen	—	's	confidence
				reliance
36.	little	men	's	following-
			around-	
				and-behind
37.	four	horses	orderly	—

象弭魚服　豈不日戒　玁狁孔棘　昔我往矣　楊柳依依　今我來思　雨雪霏霏　行道遲遲　載渴載飢　我心傷悲　莫知我哀

38.	ivory	bow-end	fish	robe
39.	how	not	daily	alert
40.	Hsien	Yün	quite (part.)	urgent
41.	formerly	I	go	(part.-exclam.)
42.	willow	—	manner of fluttering	
43.	now	I	come back	(part.)
44.	rain	snow	profuse-looking	—
45.	walk	road	slowly belatedly	—
46.	(part.)	thirsty	(part.)	hungry
47.	my	heart	worried	sad
48.	not	know	my	sorrow

1. Pick ferns, pick ferns,
2. Ferns are sprouting.
3. Return, return,
4. The year is dusking.
5. No house, no home,
6. The Hsien-yün are the sole cause.
7. No time to rest,
8. The Hsien-yün are the sole cause.
9. Pick ferns, pick ferns,
10. Ferns are soft.
11. Return, return,
12. Hearts are sorrowful.
13. Sorrowful hearts burn, burn.
14. Now hunger, now thirst.
15. Garrison here and there,
16. No message home.
17. Pick ferns, pick ferns,
18. Ferns are coarse.
19. Return, return,
20. The tenth month is here.
21. King's affairs still undone,
22. No time to rest,
23. And sorrow pierces heart.
24. We go and return not.
25. What is blooming?

26. Flowers of the cherry.
27. Whose imposing chariot?
28. The general's.
29. War-chariot is yoked,
30. Four horses so tall.
31. How dare we settle?
32. One month, three battles.
33. Ride the four horses.
34. Four horses martial in gait.
35. The general rides behind.
36. Besides them, lesser men.
37. Four horses, a grand file.
38. Ivory bow-ends,
    fish-bone arrow-holders.
39. How dare we slake?
40. The Hsien-yün are wide awake.
41. When we set out,
42. Willows dangled green.
43. Now I return,
44. Sleets in a mist.
45. We drag along.
46. Now thirst, now hunger.
47. My heart is full of sorrow.
48. Who knows? Who will know?

黄

黄行將方玄矜夫民虎野夫暇狐草車道

不不不四不不征匪匪曠征不者幽之周

草日人營草人我為兕彼我夕芃彼棧彼

何何何經何何哀獨匪率哀朝有率有行

NO. 234. WHAT GRASS NOT YELLOWED

1. what	grass plant	not	yellow
2. what	day	not	walk dispatched march
3. what	man	not	taken recruited go
4. plan attend-to	build	four	quarters
5. what	grass	not	black
6. what	man	not	sick
7. woe alas	we	recruited expeditioning	men
8. alone	be	not	men
9. not	rhinoceros ox	not	tiger
10. go-along	that	spacious desolate	wilderness
11. woe	we	recruited	men
12. morning	evening	not	leisure
13. there-is (i.e., those that have furry hair)	furry-haired	(those)	fox
14. go-along	that those	dark obscure	grass
15. there-is	bamboo-wattle lath-box	's	cars chariots
16. go	that those	Chou	trail trek

1. What grass not yellowed?
2. Which day, no march?
3. What man not taken
4. To guard the four frontiers?
5. What grass not blackened?
6. What man not sick?
7. Sorrow to the soldiers:
8. We, alone, not human?
9. Not oxen, not tigers
10. Moving along wild fields
11. Sorrow to the soldiers
12. Morning till dark, no rest.
13. Foxes up their tail
14. Moving along tall dark grass
15. We move war-carts
16. Moving along our own trek.

FROM *CH'U TZ'U* SONGS OF THE SOUTH

CH'U TZ'U

The collection *Ch'u Tz'u* (songs from the state of Ch'u in southern China) came to us through Wang I (d. A.D. 158), whose compilation and notes form the only reliable source of information on their existence. As a result, little is certain about the authorship of many of the poems therein, although most scholars believe that a number of them, particularly "Li Sao" ("Encountering Sorrow"), must have been written by Ch'ü Yüan (329–299 B.C.), a loyal minister of Ch'u driven to drown himself by his slanderers in court.

A brief examination of "Li Sao,"* after which all other Ch'u songs were modeled, will yield some striking differences from the northern collection *Shih Ching.* First of all, unlike the impersonal voices of the *Songs,* this poem begins with an unmistakable, intensely personal expression characterized by the venting of the poet's own predicament and his imaginative flight in search of models of integrity and beauty. Again, whereas in the *Songs* the anonymous poets simply use the objects most directly related to their communal experience for their "spontaneous connections and correspondences," Ch'ü Yüan, or the author of other Ch'u songs, employs a substantial amount of deliberate symbolism and allegory such as those of fragrant herbs representing virtues and the imaginative flight where different models of integrity are encountered representing quest and ideals. Even the "Nine Songs," a group of folk songs connected with shamanistic ritual performances, take on the personal stamp of Ch'ü Yüan whose purported editorship and retouching of these materials brought in extremely ornate diction and rhetorical devices alien to folk composition.

Another difference between the two collections is metrical: The *Songs* are dominantly four-character lines and the Ch'u songs are dominantly six-character lines plus the sound *hsi* (serving as a ceasura-apostrophe) placed either among or at the end of the lines in patterns like XXX hsi XX or XXXXXX hsi. The former resembles more static regulated drumbeats and the latter, surges of waves.

*Not translated here because of its length. See David Hawke's translation in *Ch'u Tz'u, The Songs of the South* (London, 1959). The present selection also contains similar traits.

54

One interesting thing about the Ch'u songs is the *flight* or *excursion* theme that bears some likeness to the epistemological search in Western poetry and yields also a similar discursive explanatory procedure. But in spite of the tremendous influence these songs had upon later poets in imagery, diction, and metrics, this procedure has never really played a central role in the poetry to come, except perhaps in the *fu* form (rhymeprose).*

*All the representative *fu* are too long to be accommodated into the present format of the book. A good selection of the Han *fu* can be found in Burton Watson's *Early Chinese Literature* (New York, 1962), pp. 254–285.

哀郢　　　　屈原

皇天之不純命兮，何百姓之震愆。
民離散而相失兮，方仲春而東遷。
去故鄉而就遠兮，遵江夏以流亡。
出國門而軫懷兮，甲之朝吾以行。
發郢都而去閭兮，怊荒忽其焉極。
楫齊揚以容與兮，哀見君而不再得。
望長楸而太息兮，涕淫淫其若霰。
過夏首而西浮兮，顧龍門而不見。
心嬋媛而傷懷兮，眇不知其所蹠。
順風波以從流兮，焉洋洋而為客。
凌陽侯之氾濫兮，忽翱翔之焉薄。

1. imperial
2. how
3. citizens
4. just
5. leave
6. follow
7. out-of off
8. Chia
9. leave
10. distantly
11. oars
12. bemoan
13. watch
14. tear
15. pass
16. look-at
17. heart
18. vaguely
19. follow
20. then
21. ride
22. suddenly

YING FROM "THE NINE DECLARATIONS"   *Chü Yüan (329?-299? B.C.)*

Heaven	's	not	just (i.e., not at its normal)	life	(caes.-apos.)
hundred family-names (i.e., the subjects)	's		fear	sin	(caes.-apos.)
scatter	separate	and	from-each-other	estranged lost	(caes.-apos.)
mid	spring	and	eastward	exiled	(caes.-apos.)
former (i.e.,homeland)	country	and	toward head-for	distance	(caes.-apos.)
Chiang	Hsia	into	exile	—	
country (i.e., city-gate)	gate	and	aching	heart	(caes.-apos.)
's	morning	I	to	go	
Ying	capital	and	depart-from	hometown	(caes.-apos.)
desolate-farness		(part.)	where	extreme destination	
in-unison	wave	to (part.)	leisurely slowly with-hesitation	—	(caes.-apos.)
seeing	prince	and	not	again	possible
long	Catalpa	and	sigh	—	(caes.-apos.)
flooding	—	(part.)	like	sleet	
surging	—				
soaking	—				
Hsia	head	and	westward	drift float	(caes.-apos.)
Dragon	Gate	and	not	see	
involved	—	and	wounded saddened	heart	(caes.-apos.)
not	know	(he) (i.e., what he)	what	tread	
wind	wave	(part.) to and	follow	stream	(caes.-apos.)
wandering	—	and	be	guest wanderer	
Yang (i.e., Wave God)	Hou	's	brimming-surge tremulous-waves	—	(caes.-apos.)
glide	soar	(part.) to	where	end stop	

心嬋媛而傷懷兮
眇不知其所蹠
順風波以從流兮
焉洋洋而為客
凌陽侯之氾濫兮
忽翱翔之焉薄
心絓結而不解兮
思蹇產而不釋
將運舟而下浮兮
上洞庭而下江
去終古之所居兮
今逍遙而來東
羌靈魂之欲歸兮
何須臾而忘反
背夏浦而西思兮
哀故都之日遠
登大墳以遠望兮
聊以舒吾憂心
哀州土之平樂兮
悲江介之遺風
當陵陽之焉至兮
淼南渡之焉如
曾不知夏之為丘兮
孰兩東門之可蕪
心不怡之長久兮
憂與愁其相接
惟郢路之遼遠兮
江與夏之不可涉

#		
23.	heart	hang
24.	thought	obsessed
25.	shall	manipulate steer
26.	up	Tung
27.	leave	extreme (i.e., leave his ancestral residence)
28.	now	wander
29.	(part.)	soul
30.	how	moment (i.e., in a moment)
31.	back	Hsia (i.e., with back against Hsia-p'u)
32.	bemoan	old
33.	ascend	big
34.	So	to
35.	bemoan	prefecture
36.	saddened-by	river
37.	when	Ling
38.	immense	south
39.	almost even	not
40.	who	two
41.	heart	not
42.	sorrow	and
43.	but	Ying
44.	Chiang	and
45.	distracted	like

knot	and	not	untie	(caes.-apos.)
—	and	not	relieve	
boat	and	downward	drift	(caes.-apos.)
T'ing	and	down	Chiang	
ancient	's	where	inhabit	(caes.-apos.)
—	and	come	east	
—	's	desiring	return	(caes.-apos.)
—	and	forget	return	
P'u	and	westward	think	(caes.-apos.)
capital	's	daily	farther	
embankment	to	distantly	watch	(caes.-apos.)
comfort soothe	my	worried	heart	
land	's	wide-expanse	affluence	(caes.-apos.)
side	's	passed-down	folkways	
Yang	(part.)	where	go	(caes.-apos.)
sailing	(part.)	how	go	(caes.-apos.)
know	big-house	's	becoming	mound (caes.-apos.)
east	gates	's	can	leave-desolate full of weeds
pleasant	(part.)	longtime	—	(caes.-apos.)
sorrow	(they)	with-each-other	join	(caes.-apos.)
road	's	remote	—	(caes.-apos.)
Hsia	's	not- able-to impossible-to	wade	
go	not	believe		(caes.-apos.)*

*Away from home yet it seems not—distracted as in a dream, to believe it? not to believe it?

今不通感兮 約持進之行天 妒佽美慨進遞 觀峙兮 鄉丘而 棄之 逐兮

復兮　兮　兮　兮　名兮　兮　兮

信而不含之而 難頷郫抗薄 嫉之慈之之而 流之故首罪而忘

不年而而之而 之而之而 慈之之而 何

去九鬱傑歡豹港離舜者人不倫人蹊遠 目反反必吾夜

若今鬱佗承洼湛被堯者讒以慍夫踐超曰 余壹飛宛非日

怨至慘褰外謇忠妒彼曒眾被憎妒眾美亂曼箕鳥狐信何

46. until
47. sadly
48. obstructed

49. outside appearance
50. really

51. loyal

52. jealousy
53. those
54. high-and-remote
55. all
56. dub
57. hate

58. love

59. majority
60. beauty

61. run
62. wish
63. bird
64. fox
65. actually
66. which

now	nine	years	and		not/return
melancholy	—	and	not	communicate	(caes.-apos.)
despair	—	and	keep-in-mouth	sorrow	
court	favor	's	flattering	—	(caes.-apos.)
weak-and-fragile	—	and	hard-to	withhold	
firmly	—	and	is-willing	present devote	(caes.-apos.)
flourishing	—	and	obstruct	(him, me)	(caes.-apos.)
Yao	Shun	's	profound	deed	(caes.-apos.)
—	and	reach	heaven		
slanderer	—	's	jealousy	—	(caes.-apos.)
with	not	humane	's	false	name
suppressed-feelings	wishing-to-make-known	's	slender	beauty	(caes.-apos.)
(part.)	man	's	flattering-bombast	—	
scuttling	—	and	daily	advance	(caes.-apos.)
detached	distant	and	increasingly	become-farther	
	Envoi				
my	eyes	to	scan	sight	(caes.-apos.)
one	return	but	what	time	
fly	return	old	country		
die	always	pillow	hill		
not	my	fault	but	abandoned	exiled
day	night	but	forget	(it)	

61

1. Unjust, Imperial Heaven's way:
2. How the commons were shocked and tried!
3. People scattered, separated, lost.
4. Middle of spring: eastward exodus began.
5. Away, hometown! Toward distant lands!
6. Along rivers Chiang and Hsia into exile!
7. Outside the city gate, my heart was stricken.
8. In the morning of the *chia* day, I departed
9. From Capital Ying, leaving my village behind.
10. What distance? O Where to end?
11. Oars in unison yet with hesitation.
12. Sad it is not to see the prince again.
13. I looked at tall catalpas and sighed.
14. Tears, surging, drip, drip like sleets.
15. I passed the head of Hsia, floating west.
16. Looking back: where, the Dragon Gate?
17. Swelling with longing, my breast ached
18. No knowing what step next and where.
19. I coast winds and waves, following their flow.
20. Endless drift for a traveler
21. Riding the brimming surge of the Wave God!
22. A sudden upward flight, but where to rest?
23. Heart netted and knotted: no way to undo.
24. Thought all tangled: no release.
25. I let go my boat to float downward,
26. Up Lake Tung-t'ing toward the big Chiang,
27. Away from my house of century old.
28. Now, wobbling, east, farther east
29. While my soul stirred, longing for return,
30. Not for a moment did I forget return!
31. Back against Hsia P'u, my thought ran west.
32. All the Capital farther day by day!
33. I climbed atop an embankment, viewing the distance
34. So as to ease my heart meshed with pain.
35. Ai! such fertile soil, these towns, villages.
36. Sad to remember folkways by the River's bank.
37. Already at Ling-yang, where else to go?
38. Immense water: cross to the South? then what?
39. Not knowing the palace now turned mounds.
40. How to believe the two East Gates all weed-grown!

41. Long time my heart has been out of tune
42. Sorrow upon sorrow.
43. But the road to Ying is remote!
44. The Chiang and Hsia so difficult to cross!
45. Believing it not believing it
46. Nine years and not return!
47. Grief densely interwoven: no break, no path.
48. Prisoned in despair: only sorrow to bite.
49. Rhetoric and charm to win imperial favor
50. Were signs of weak and infirm labor.
51. Profound loyalty seeks expression again and again
52. Finds itself blocked, broken or bent.
53. Great deeds of model rulers Yao and Shun
54. Whose sublime thoughts brightened stars and sun
55. Are dimmed by slanderers' clever design
56. To call them false names: the Great Unkind.
57. Thus, he hates virtues from extensive ken
58. And prefers empty loud claims of small men.
59. The crowd jostle forward day by day
60. While Beauty is banished far far away.
    Envoi
61. I run my eyes over the distance around me,
62. Longing to return, but when?
63. Flown birds return their nests.
64. Dying foxes head for their mounds.
65. This exile, believe me, is no crime of my own doing.
66. Days and nights, I can never for one moment forget.

YÜEH-FU; NINETEEN ANCIENT POEMS

How did the rulers of ancient China learn of the hopes and fears, joys and disappointments of the common people? Since the Ch'in Dynasty (221–205 B.C.) or earlier, there existed an official organ called *Yüeh Fu,* "Music Bureau," which collected ballad-songs from different provinces and through which reactions to the government could be detected. *Shih Ching* was believed to have come into existence in a similar manner. But it was not until 125 B.C., when Emperor Wu of the Han Dynasty revived this organization, that the term *Yüeh Fu* ceased to become merely the designation of an imperial office. *Yüeh-fu* has since come to mean the collection of poems and the name of a genre.

These popular ballad-songs were originally preserved with their accompanying music that is now lost. Many of the traces of their musical relationship can still be found in repetitions, borrowed stanzas, and cliché formulas scattered among these written texts. Compare the two variations of "The East Gate" in the present selection: a change of music in different dynasties demands additional words to fill out the measure. Examples abound in the original *Yüeh-fu* collection. Note also whole lines borrowed from other songs. The last two lines in "Sad Song" ("All swallowed in thought: no speech / Inside the guts, wheels grind and turn") appear intact in "Old Song." Other lines in the latter, ("Home: each day farther away / Girdle: each day becomes looser") appear, with only slight variations, in No. 1 of the "Nineteen Ancient Songs" ("Separation: each day farther away / My girdle: each day becomes looser"), "Nineteen Ancient Poems" being a group of works apparently crystallized from influences of other current examples of *Yüeh-fu.* These same lines might have been taken from other earlier uncollected ballad-songs.

Although both were of folk origin, the *Yüeh-fu* ballad-songs differ from those in *Shih Ching* in many noticeable ways. Many of the *Yüeh-fu* songs appear more independent as lyrics than those in *Shih Ching* in the sense that the latter was under greater subordination to musical pressure. In the repetition of stanzas in *Shih Ching,* we find only minimal variations in meaning. In contrast, fewer stanzaic repetitions of this kind are found in the *Yüeh-fu* and when such repetitions happen, much more meaningful variations are introduced and they tend to build up progressively toward a climax. This fact, no doubt, indicates also that the songs must have been very consciously worked over by poet-musicians.

Another obvious difference is in the line length. The *Yüeh-fu* songs are predominantly five-character lines, the beginning of the fundamental line length for the poetry of many centuries to come. A comparison with the predominantly four-character lines in *Shih Ching* will reveal that the four-character line-structure does not have the same compactness and variety of function of the five-character line-structure because the extra fifth character, when placed between the other four characters or at the end, would help to connect, modify, and complicate the relationship between the remaining two pairs of characters that often form compounds. While, in this historical juncture, there was little effort to hammer and sharpen this extra fifth character to yield a multiple suggestiveness or to form what was later to be called the "eye" of the line, the rise of the five-character line-structure was an important stylistic turn in Chinese poetry. Following the steady "hammering" of the third-, fourth-, and fifth-century poets, the T'ang and Sung writers had made a great art of this added character.

The group designated as "Nineteen Ancient Poems" was probably composed between the two Han Dynasties (Former Han 206 B.C.–A.D. 25; Later Han A.D. 25–220) by poet-musicians who turned the *Yüeh-fu* lines into his own artistic manipulation. Already, we find compact and concise buildup of line-power of a kind admired by many later poets, and upon which they modeled their poetry, including the T'ang master Li Po.

Thematically, the *Yüeh-fu* songs are also distinctively different. Here are some of the recurring motifs: sorrow in separation caused by war; exile and poverty, victimized by the wreckage of time; bleakness of the frontier; return of an old man from war finding everything in ruins; tortuous trip; miseries brought about by war; return of a wanderer—all oriented toward social problems. Little communal ceremonial living is reflected, although the southern *Yüeh-fu*, mostly love poems, would spill a trickle every now and then of the charm of unretouched songs.

The extensive imitation of these songs has given rise to what is appropriately called literary *Yüeh-fu*, the sophisticated use of which parallels the literary use of the English ballads. A chart of the approximate development of the *Yüeh-fu* may be useful here:

Year	Dynasty	Han-style	Southern-style
206 B.C–A.D. 220	2 Hans	original	
A.D. 220–316	Wei, Chin	imitation (literary)	
317–588	Six Dynasties	imitation (literary)	original
589–	Sui, T'ang		imitation (literary)

行行重行行　與君生別離
相去萬餘里　各在天一涯
道路阻且長　會面安可知
胡馬依北風　越鳥巢南枝
相去日已遠　衣帶日已緩
浮雲蔽白日　遊子不顧返
思君令人老　歲月忽已晚
棄捐勿復道　努力加餐飯

NO. I. WALK ON AGAIN WALK ON

1.	walk	walk	again	walk	walk
2.	with from	you	alive	separate	—
3.	mutual (distance between)	go	ten-thousand	odd	mile/s
4.	each	at	sky/s	one	end
5.	road/s	—	difficult	and	long
6.	meeting	—	how	possible	know
7.	Tartar	horse/s	follow	north	wind/s
8.	Yueh	bird/s	nest	south	branch/es
9.	(distance between)		each-day	already	distant
10.	girdle	—	each-day	already	loose
11.	floating	cloud/s	cover	white	sun
12.	wanderer	—	not	care	return
13.	think (of)	you	make	people	old
14.	year	month	suddenly	already	late
15.	abandoned	—	not	again	mention
16.	industriously	—	add	meal/s	—

1. Walk on again walk on.
2. From you, separated alive.
3. Between us, a million odd miles,
4. Each at one end of the sky.
5. The roads are difficult and long.
6. To meet: where, how and when?
7. Tartar horses follow north winds.
8. Birds of Yueh nest on south branches.
9. Separation: each day farther away.
10. My girdle: each day becomes looser.
11. Floating clouds veil the white sun.
12. The wanderer: no thought to return.
13. Thinking of you makes me old.
14. Months, years: all of a sudden: dusk.
15. Forget it! Say no more!
16. With redoubled effort, eat, eat.

青鬱盈皎娥纖昔今蕩空
青鬱盈皎娥纖為子林
青鬱盈當紅出倡蕩行難
河園樓當紅出倡蕩行難
畔中上窗粉素家子不獨
草柳女孀妝手女婦歸守

NO. 3. GREEN BEYOND GREEN, THE GRASS ALONG THE RIVER

1. green	green	river	bank	grass
2. dense	dense	garden	middle	willow
3. full (first bloom of youth)	full	storey (i.e., girl on tower)	on	girl
4. bright	bright	at	window	
5. fair	fair	red (rouge)	powder	toilet
6. slender	slender	put forth	white	hand
7. formerly	is/was	singing	house	girl
8. now	is	wandering (playboy)	man's	wife
9. wandering (playboy)	man	go-away	not	return
10. empty	bed	hard	alone	keep

Experimental version

1. Green beyond green, the grass along the river.
2. Leaves on leaves, willows in the garden.
3. Bloom of bloom, the girl up in the tower.
4. A ball of brightness at the windowsill.
5. A flash of fairness in her rouged face.
6. Slender, she put forth a slender white hand.
7. She was a singing girl before.
8. Now wife of a playboy.
9. The playboy went and never returned.
10. Empty bed! Alone! How hard it is to keep.

疎親視壙田薪風人閭囚
以以茸與禹禹悲殺里無
日日門丘罕攉多愁故道
者者郭見墓柏楊蕭還歸
去来出但古松白蕭思欲

NO. 14. THOSE GONE ARE DAY BY DAY REMOTE

1.	gone (what is gone)	thing	day-by-day	already	remote (in affection)
2.	coming (what is coming)	thing	day-by-day	already	near (in affection)
3.	out	gate-door (outer-wall-of-city)		straight	see
4.	but	see	hill/s	and	mound/s
5.	ancient	grave/s	plow	into	field/s
6.	pine/s	cypress/es	demolish	into	firewood
7.	white	poplar/s	much	sorrowful	wind
8.	*hsiao-hsiao* (onomatopoeic)		sad	kill	man
9.	think (of)	return	old	hometown	—
10.	want	return	road	no	track

1. Those gone are day by day remote.
2. Those coming are day by day near.
3. Straight view outside the gate:
4. Mounds and mounds and mounds.
5. Ancient graves plowed into fields.
6. Pines, cypresses axed into firewood.
7. From white poplars, much sorrowful wind.
8. Comes swish-swish cutting men.
9. Longing to return home
10. Longing, and finding no road

FROM THE *YÜEH-FU* COLLECTION

OF BALLAD-SONGS OF THE BUREAU

OF MUSIC IN THE HAN DYNASTY

上邪

上邪
我欲與君相知
長命無絕衰
山無陵
江水為竭
冬雷震震
夏雨雪
天地合
乃敢與君絕

O HEAVENS!

1.	above	(part.-exclam.)			
2.	I	desire want to	with	you	each-other know love
3.	long (i.e., long life life long)	life	not	cease-	decrease
4.	mountain	no	range		
5.	river	water	(as-to)	dry-up	
6.	winter	thunder	chen	chen (onomatopoeic)	
7.	summer	rain (v.)	snow		
8.	heaven sky	earth	close merge		
9.	then	dare	with	you	break

1. O Heavens!
2. I want to stick with you
3. Long life together and no break
4. Only when mountains are no mountains
5. Rivers are without water
6. Winter comes thundering
7. Summer snowing
8. Only when sky and earth merge
9. Would I break with you

有　　所　　思

南君篸之心之灰，其往思君吠知之。秋夬高知之。

有所思，乃在大海南。
何用問遺君，雙珠瑇瑁簪，用玉紹繚之。
聞君有他心，拉雜摧燒之。
摧燒之，當風揚其灰。
從今以往，勿復相思，相思與君絕。
雞鳴狗吠，兄嫂當知之。
［妃呼狶］，
秋風肅肅晨風颸，東方須臾高知之。

HIM I'M THINKING OF

1.	there-is	(what)	think-of			
2.	is	in	big	sea	south	
3.	what	with	to-pay-regards	to-give-as-gifts	you	
4.	two double	pearl/s	tortoise	—	hairpin pin	
5.	with	jade	intertwine	—	it	
6.	hear	you	have	other	heart	
			(i.e., take fancy on someone else)			
7.	pull	mix	smash	burn	it	
8.	—	—	smash	burn	it	
9.	in	wind	let-fly	its	ash	
10.	from	now	on	—		
11.	not	again	of-each-other	think		
12.	of-each-other	think thinking	with	you	sever	
13.	rooster cock	crow	dog	bark		
14.	elder-brother	elder sister-in-law	will	know	it	
15.	alas (onomatopoeic)	—	—			
16.	autumn	wind	shu shu (onomatopoeic)	shu	morning pheasant	wind —	fast
17.	eastern	side	presently	—	dawn	know	it

1. Him I'm thinking of
2. Who lives south of the big sea
3. What to send him as a gift?
4. Two pearls worked into a tortoise-shell pin
5. Intertwined with jade
6. I heard he is unfaithful
7. I angrily break and burn it
8. Break and burn it
9. And let the wind blow away its ashes
10. From now on
11. No thought of him
12. No more–the end with him
13. Cocks crow; dogs bark
14. My brother and wife would then know
15. Alas! alas!
16. Autumn winds whistle. Bird-of-morning-wind sings
17. When the east brightens, I then would know . . . .

江南

江南可採蓮
蓮葉何田田
魚戲蓮葉間
魚戲蓮葉東
魚戲蓮葉西
魚戲蓮葉南
魚戲蓮葉北

SOUTH OF THE YANGTZE

1.	river	south	can	pick	lotus
2.	lotus	leaves	how	drifting	drifting
3.	fish	sport	lotus	leaves	middle
4.	fish	sport	lotus	leaves	east
5.	fish	sport	lotus	leaves	west
6.	fish	sport	lotus	leaves	south
7.	fish	sport	lotus	leaves	north

1. South of the river: to pluck lotus.
2. Lotus leaves drift, drift.
3. Fish sport, midst of lotus leaves:
4. Fish sport, east of lotus-leaves.
5. Fish sport, west of lotus-leaves.
6. Fish sport, south of lotus-leaves.
7. Fish sport, north of lotus-leaves.

戰城南

戰城南，死郭北，野死不葬烏可食。

為我謂烏：且為客豪！野死諒不葬，腐肉安能去子逃？

水深激激，蒲葦冥冥；梟騎戰鬥死，駑馬徘徊鳴。

梁築室，何以南？何以北？禾黍不穫君何食？願為忠臣安可得？

思子良臣，良臣誠可思：朝行出攻，暮不夜歸。

FIGHTING SOUTH OF THE RAMPARTS

1. Fighting, south of the ramparts.
2. Death, north of the wall.
3. Death in the wilds: no burial, for crows to feast.
4. Go tell the crows:
5. "Mourn for these soldiers first.
6. Death in the wilds and no burial:
7. Can their rotten flesh escape you?"
8. Deep water roars.
9. Dense reeds darken.
10. Riders fight to death.
11. Horses whine back and forth.
12. Houses on bridges.
13. How, to south?
14. How, to north?
15. Ears of grains left unharvested, what can the lord eat?
16. To be loyal, though willing, but how?
17. Thinking of you, good soldiers,
18. Good soldiers worthy of thinking:
19. Morning: to fight.
20. Dusk till night: no return.

THE EAST GATE

東門行

出東門
不顧歸
来入門
悵欲悲
盎中無斗米儲
還視架上無懸衣
拔劍東門去
舍中兒母牽衣啼
他家但願富貴
賤妾與君共餔糜
上用倉浪天故
下當用此黃口兒
今非
咄
行
吾去為遲
白髮時下難久居

1. out of
2. not
3. come
4. at-a-loss

5. basin
6. backward
7. pull
8. house

9. other
10. humble (i.e., I)
11. up
12. down
13. now
14. bah
    alas
15. go
16. I

17. white

east	gate				
think-of	return				
enter	door				
about-to	sorrow				
bordering-on					
middle	no	peck-of-	rice	storage	
look	cloth-hanger	on	no	hung	clothes
sword	east	gate	go		
middle	son/'s (i.e., wife)	mother	pull	clothes	weep
family	but	wish-for	wealth	rank	
concubine	with	you	share	gruel	
for	blue	wave	sky	sake	
for	yellow	mouth	little	son	
wrong					
go	(part.) being	late			
hair	often	fall	difficult	long	live

The East Gate (original lyric)*

1. Out of East Gate:
2. No more thought of returning.
3. Returning to the door:
4. Heart rent by distress.
5. In the crock, no rice.
6. Upon the peg, no hanging clothes.
7. Thereupon he drew a sword and to the East Gate!
8. His wife pulled at his hem, and weeping:
9. "Others aim at gold and rank.
10. I am content to have gruel with you.

*This translation is based on the authoritative reading of this poem by Yü Kuan-ying (see *Yüeh-fu shih-hsüan* [1954], p. 30).

11. Mark above the blue-seething sky
12. And below, the yellow face of this child.
13. Now this move: wrong"
14. "Bah !
15. Away!
16. Otherwise it will be too late!
17. White hair already falling, to survive, how hard!"

Variation To Chin Dynasty Music

Out of the East Gate:
No more thought of returning.
Returning to the door:
Heart rent by distress.
In the crock, no rice.

Upon the rack, no hanging clothes
Thereupon he drew a sword and to the East Gate!
The child's mother pulled at his hem, weeping:
"Others aim at gold and rank.
I am content to have gruel with you.
                                        gruel with you.

Mark above the blue-seething sky
And below the yellow face of this child.
Now in time of peace
No break of law
Love yourself and do no wrong!

Now in time of peace
No break of law
Love yourself and do no wrong!"
"Away !
Otherwise it will be too late!"
"Go safely
And come home!"

悲歌

悲 歌 可 以 當 泣
遠 望 可 以 當 歸
思 念 故 鄉 　 人 船
鬱 鬱 家 無 言 轉
歸 渡 河 無 能 輪
思 不 車
心 中
腸

SAD SONG

1.	sad	song	may	—	substitute serve-as	weeping
2.	distant	look	may	—	substitute	return
3.	think	miss	old (i.e., hometown)	country		
4.	melancholy dense	— —	listless cluttered	— —		
5.	desire	return	home	no	man	
6.	desire	cross	river	no	boat	
7.	heart's	thought	cannot	—	utter	
8.	guts	middle	cart	wheel	turn	

1. Sad song for weeping.
2. Looking into the distance for homebound trip.
3. Thinking of hometown:
4. Densely-meshed, clods and clusters within.
5. To return: nobody at home.
6. To cross the river: no boat.
7. All swallowed in thought: no speech.
8. Inside the guts, wheels grind and turn.

古歌

悠悠殺人

蕭蕭愁殺人　人憂頭颮修趨趨能輪　風修遠緩言轉

秋風亦亦中不我地木家帶思中

秋出入座誰令胡樹離衣心腸

OLD SONG

1.	autumn	wind	hsiao (onomatopoeic)	hsiao	sorrow	kill	man
2.	out	also	sorrow grief			
3.	in	also	sorrow grief			
4.	seat	middle	what	man		
5.	who	not	harbor	sorrow		
6.	make	me	white	head		
7.	Tartar	land	plenty	stormy	wind	
8.	tree	—	how	slender	slender	
9.	leave	home	daily	tend	far	
10.	clothes	belt	daily	tend	loose	
11.	heart's	thought	cannot	—	utter	
12.	guts	middle	cart	wheel	turn	

1. Autumn winds, swish-swish, sorrow killing men.
2. Going out: sorrow
3. Coming in: sorrow
4. Who among us
5. Is not distressed?
6. Makes me white-headed:
7. Fierce winds, in blankets, over Tartar land.
8. Trees, drooping, how dead!
9. Home: each day farther away.
10. Girdle: each day becomes looser.
11. All swallowed in thought: no speech
12. Inside the guts, wheels grinds and turn.

征

征歸人誰家纍入飛穀葵飴羹熟誰看衣
軍軍得里阿君粟實上旅旅作作時阿向我
從從鄉有是家狗梁生生持持一貽東沾
五五十逢中看柏從從庭上穀葵飴知門落
十十八道家遙松冤雉中井舂捺羹不出淚

1.	fifteen	—	join	army	go-on-an-expedition
2.	eighty	—	then	able-to	return
3.	way	meet	village	district	man
4.	home	middle	there-is	(part.)	who
5.	from-a-distance	look	is	your	home
6.	pine	cypress	mound	clustered	clustered
7.	rabbit	from	dog	hole	enter
8.	pheasant	from	rafter	on/above	fly
9.	middle	yard	grow	wild	grain
10.	well	on; upon	grow	wild	mallow
11.	beat grind	grain	for/ hold	make	rice
12.	pick	mallow	for/ hold	make	soup
13.	soup	rice	one	time	cooked
14.	not	know	give	(part.)	who
15.	go-out-of	door	east-ward	face	watch
16.	tears	drop	drench	my	clothes

1. At fifteen I went to war.
2. At eighty now I made it home.
3. Meeting one from my village:
4. "Who now is at home?"
5. "Over there is your house."
6. Pines, cypresses, tombs in clusters.
7. Rabbits come in from dog-holes.
8. Pheasants fly upon the beams.
9. Middle of court: wild grains rise.
10. Well's edge: wild mallows grow.
11. Grind grains to make rice.
12. Pick mallows to make soup.
13. Rice and soup soon ready.
14. But for whom?
15. Go to the east gate to look out:
16. Tears drench my clothes.

飲馬長城窟行

青青河畔草　綿綿思遠道
遠道不可思　宿昔夢見之
夢見在我傍　忽覺在他鄉
他鄉各異縣　展轉不相見
枯桑知天風　海水知天寒
入門各自媚　誰肯相為言
客從遠方來　遺我雙鯉魚
呼兒烹鯉魚　中有尺素書
長跪讀素書　書中竟何如
上言加餐食　下言長相憶

1. green	green	river	side	grass
2. uninterrupted on-and-on	—	think-of	distant	way
3. distant	way	cannot	—	think-of
4. previous	night	dream	see	him
5. dream	see	at	my	side
6. suddenly	feel	in	other	land country
7. other	land country	each	different	district
8. toss	turn	cannot	mutual	see
9. withering withered	mulberry	know	heaven sky	wind
10. sea	water	know	weather heaven; sky	cold
11. enter	door	each	self	flatter elated
12. who	would willing	each-other	(for)—	speak
13. guest	from	far	side	come
14. leave	me	pair (i.e., letter)	carp	fish
15. call	child	"cook"	carp	—
16. middle	there-is	a-Chinese-yard	silk	note
17. long (to kneel with laps and upper part of one's body upright)	kneel	read	silk	note
18. note	middle	after-all	what (what about)	like
19. above (i.e., the first part)	there-is	increase	meal	food
20. below (i.e., the last part)	there-is	long	of-each-other	miss; think

1. Green upon green, grass along the river.
2. On and on: thinking into the distance.
3. The distance: not possible to think.
4. Last night I dreamed of him,
5. Dreamed of him by my side
6. To find him, suddenly, in other lands.
7. Other lands: he and I at different ends.
8. Thinking—mind-tossed—see not.
9. Withering mulberries sense cutting winds.
10. Sea water knows too well the cold.
11. Among those returning elated
12. Who, to spare a word with me?
13. A visitor came from distant lands
14. Left me "a pair of carps"*
15. I asked my child to "cook" them
16. To find in them a letter in silk
17. I kneeled straight to read it
18. What, one asks, is in the letter?
19. It begins: *Eat, eat and eat.*
20. *Remember, yet remember,* it ends.

*i.e., letters

陌上桑

日出東南隅
照我秦氏樓
秦氏有好女
自名為羅敷
羅敷善蠶桑
採桑城南隅
青絲為籠係
桂枝為籠鈎
頭上倭墮髻
耳中明月珠
緗綺為下裙
紫綺為上襦
行者見羅敷
下擔捋髭鬚
少年見羅敷
脫帽著帩頭
耕者忘其犁

鋤者忘其鋤來歸相怨怒但坐觀羅敷使君從南來五馬立踟躕使君遣吏往問是誰家姝秦氏有好女自名為羅敷羅敷年幾何二十尚不足十五頗有餘使君謝羅敷寧可共載不羅敷前致辭使君一何愚使君自有婦羅敷自有夫

東方千餘騎夫婿居上頭何用識夫婿白馬從驪駒青絲繫馬尾黃金絡馬頭腰中鹿盧劍可值千萬餘十五府小史二十朝大夫三十侍中郎四十專城居為人潔白皙鬑鬑頗有鬚盈盈公府步冉冉府中趨坐中數千人皆言夫婿殊

BALLAD OF THE MULBERRY ROAD

I

1. The sun rises in the southeast corner,
2. Shining upon the chambers of our Ch'ins.
3. In them a pretty girl.
4. Self-named Lo-fu.
5. Lo-fu loves silkworms and mulberry trees.
6. She plucks leaves south of the walls.
7. Green silk for her basket trappings.
8. Cassia bough for her basket handle.
9. On her head, a dangling plait.
10. At her ears, bright moon pearls.
11. Yellow satin for her skirt beneath.
12. Purple satin for her short-coat above.
13. Passersby seeing Lo-fu
14. Put down their loads to twirl their mustaches and beard.
15. Young men seeing Lo-fu
16. Take off their hats to redo their head-dresses.
17. Farmers forget their ploughs.
18. Hoemen forget their hoes.
19. When they get home they are all irritated
20. After having watched Lady Lo-fu.

II

21. From the south comes the Prefect.
22. His five horses falter their pace.
23. The Prefect sends an officer over
24. To ask whose daughter she can be.
25. "In the chamber of Ch'in the pretty girl
26. Self named Lo-fu."
27. "How old, tell me, is this Lo-fu?"
28. "Not quite twenty
29. But well past her teens."
30. The Prefect sends words to Lo-fu:
31. "Would you ride together with me?"
32. Lo-fu walks up and to him says:
33. "How unthinking you are!
34. Just as you have your wife,
35. I, too, have my husband."

III

36. "From the east, a thousand horses.
37. My husband rides at the head.
38. How to tell my husband?
39. White steed followed by black colt,
40. Green silk hangs from its tail,
41. Gold trappings upon its head.
42. At his waist, a windlass sword
43. Worthy of million pieces of gold.
44. At fifteen, he became a page.
45. At twenty, he attended court.
46. At thirty, among the emperor's council.
47. At forty, assigned to govern a city.
48. He is a man, clean and white
49. With quite some beard.
50. Stately, he walks to the Prefecture.
51. Proudly, he steps back and forth.
52. Seated there, several thousand men.
53. All say my husband the finest of all."

LITERARY *YÜEH-FU*

INCLUDING POEMS INSPIRED

BY THIS GENRE

苦寒行　　　曹操

山巍屈摧發悲蹲啼民罪息懷鬱歸絕徊路

行巍詰之蕭正我路人霏嘆所怫東梁徘故

太何坂爲何聲對夾少何長多何一橋正失

上者腸輪木風羆豹谷落頸行心欲深路惑

北艱羊車樹北熊虎豁雪延遠我思水中迷

BITTER COLD: A SONG *Ts'ao Ts'ao (155–220)*

1. north	up	T'ai	Heng	Mountain
2. difficult	(part.)	how	lofty	lofty
3. goat (i.e., rugged road)	guts	slope	twisted	—
4. cart	wheel	therefore	—	break
5. trees	—	how	*hsiao-* (onomatopoeic) desolate	*she* —
6. north	wind	sound	now	sad
7. bear/s	female-bear/s	face	me	squat
8. tiger/s	leopard/s	line	road	growl
9. valley	—	few	people	—
10. snow	fall	how	dense	—
11. crane	neck	long	sigh	—
12. far long	walk trip	much	(what)	remember
13. my	heart	how	distressed	melancholy
14. think	desire	once	eastward	return
15. water	deep	bridge	—	cut-off
16. middle	road	now	pace-back-and-forth	—
17. bewildered	—	lose	old	road

棲遠飢薪麋詩哀
宿已曉取作山栽
無日同行持東使
暮行馬橐冰彼悠
薄行人擔斧悲悠

18. dusk	—	no	lodging	stop
19. walk	walk	daily day-by-day	already	far
20. man	horse	same	time	feel-hungry
21. bear	knapsack	walk	take	firewood
22. ax	ice	use	make	gruel
23. bemoan	that	East	Mountain	poem
24. distant think	distant think	make	me	sad

1. Go north up the T'ai-heng Mountains
2. How rugged, how steep!
3. Sheep-Gut Slope so tortuous,
4. Wheels are broken apart.
5. Trees whistle, so chilling.
6. North winds blow sorrowfully.
7. Bears, in ambush, attack.
8. Tigers, leopards howl from both sides.
9. In the glen, few people.
10. Snow falls, a drift of catkins.
11. I crane my neck, a long sigh.
12. Distant trip swells with memories.
13. How meshed my sad heart!
14. I desire to return east
15. Deep water and no bridge.
16. Midway, I pace back and forth
17. Bewildered, having lost my road
18. Dusk and no place to stay
19. On, on farther day by day
20. Rider and horse, both hungry
21. Pick branches for firewood
22. Ax ice to make gruel
23. Sad, the song "Return to East Mountain"*
24. Resounding deep into my grief.

*A poem from *Shih Ching* with this note in the Preface:
"The Duke of Chou returned from an expedition at the
end of three years, rewarded and commended his men.
Some great officer, in admiration of him, made this poem."

飲馬長城窟行　陳琳

飲馬長城窟，水寒傷馬骨。
往謂長城吏，慎莫稽留太原卒。
官作自有程，舉築諧汝聲。
男兒寧當格鬥死，何能怫郁築長城。
長城何連連，連連三千里。
邊城多健少，內舍多寡婦。
作書與內舍，便嫁莫留住。
善事新姑嫜，時時念我故夫子。
報書往邊地，君今出語一何鄴。
身在禍難中，何為稽留他家子。

WATER THE

1. water (v.)
2. water
3. go
4. careful
5. official
6. lift
7. male
   (i.e.,
   young men)
8. how
9. long
10. continuous

11. wall
12. inner
   (i.e., home)
13. make
14. immediately
15. well

16. time

17. rush
18. you
19. body
20. what

HORSES AT A BREACH IN THE GREAT WALL   *Ch'en Lin (?–217)*

horse/s	long (Great Wall)	wall/'s	breach		
cold	hurt	horse/'s	bone		
speak-to	long	wall	official		
not	detain	—	T'ai	Yüan	soldiers
act	by-itself	there-is	order		
build	harmonize	your	voice		
sons	rather	should	strike	battle	die

can	depressed	melancholy	build	long	wall
wall	how	continuous	—		
—	three	thousand	Chinese-miles		
side	many	strong	youths		
dwelling	many	widows	—		

letter	to	inner	dwelling		
marry	not	retain	stay		
treat	new	aunt (i.e., sisters-and brothers-in-law)	uncle	mother in-law	
time	remember	me (i.e., husband	old	husband	son
letter	to	border	land		
now	utter	words	(part.)	how	mean
in	disaster	hardship	middle		
for	retain	—	other	family's	son (i.e., daughter-in-law)

生男慎莫舉
生女哺用脯
君獨不見長城下
死人骸骨相撑拄
結髮行事君
慊慊心意關
明知邊地苦
賤妾何能久自全

21. give-birth-to
22. give-birth-to
23. you
24. dead

25. tie-up
    (i.e., marriage)
26. begrudging
    dissatisfied
    sad
27. clearly
28. humble
    (=myself)

male	careful	do-not	raise		
female	feed	with	meat		
alone	not	see	long	wall	below
men	bones	—	against-each-other	support	pillar (v.)
hair	act	serve	you		
begrudging dissatisfied sad	heart	feeling	middle		
know	border	land	hard		
concubine	how	can	long	self	preserve

1. *Water the horses at a breach in the Great Wall.*
2. *Water is cold; it hurts the horses' bones.*
3. They to the officer in charge:
4. "Don't delay our return to T'ai-yüan!"
5. "Government work has set time limits.
6. Heave-ho! Go build, go build."
7. "As men, we rather die fighting in battles.
8. How, heart-cluttered, to build the Great Wall?"
9. How the Great Wall stretches on!
10. Stretches three thousand miles beyond.
11. At the border, many many strong youths.
12. Back at home, many wives living alone.
13. Letters home to the wives:
14. "Go get married. Don't wait.
15. Be nice to your new mother-in-law.
16. And do think of me at the borders."
17. Letters to the border towns:
18. "How could you use such words!"
19. "But we are in times of distress.
20. What right do I have to retain you?
21. *When a boy is born, raise him not.*
22. *When a girl is born, feed her with meat.*
23. Do you not see beneath the Great Wall
24. Bones holding up bones of dead men?
25. "Marriage means to serve you
26. Sad no doubt I am.
27. Now that you are suffering at the borders
28. How can your humble wife live long?"

植 曹　　篇　　嗟　　吁

（曹植　吁嗟篇）

蓬然逝閒陌阡起間路淵出田北西依存澤山處難草燔痛連

轉獨根休七九風雲天沈我中更反何復八五恒所林火不荄

此何本無經越回入終下接彼而而當而周歷無吾中野豈株

嗟世去夜西北遇我謂然飆歸南東宕亡颻翩轉知為隨滅與

吁居長夙東南卒吹自忽驚故當謂宕忽飄連流誰願秋糜願

WOE INDEED!   *Ts'ao Chih (192–232)*

1. alas — —
2. living — world (i.e., how it could be otherwise)
3. Long-time — part (v.)
4. day — night
5. east — west
6. south — north
7. suddenly — meet
8. blow — me
9. self — think / say
10. suddenly — —
11. frightening — storm
12. still — return / therefore
13. should — south
14. think — east
15. floating / drifting — — / —
16. suddenly — perish / disappear
17. floating — —
18. uninterrupted — fly
19. flow — tumble
20. who — know
21. wish — be
22. autumn — follow
23. mashing — destruction
24. wish — with

this	turning	tumbleweed
how	alone	so
root	—	die
no	rest	leisure
pass	seven	east-west-bound-path
cross	nine	north-south-bound-path
whirling	wind	rise
enter	cloud	midst
end	heaven	road
down	sunken	fountain
take	me	out
that	middle	field
but	further	north
but	on-the-contrary	west
should	what	depend lean-on
but	suddenly	exist remain
round	Eight	Lakes
through	Five	Mountains
going-through		
no	constant	place residence
my	bitterness	hardship
middle	forest	grass
wild	fire	burn
how	not	painful
root	—	connect

1. Woe indeed, this tumbleweed!
2. In this world all alone.
3. Long parted from my root,
4. Day and night, no rest.
5. To east, to west, across thousand paths.
6. To north, to south, over million roads.
7. A whirlwind rises all at once
8. Blow me into the clouds
9. Is this the reach of sky?
10. Only to find myself in the abyss
11. A sudden gust bears me out
12. And send me to midfield
13. To south and yet it's north.
14. Say east and yet it's west.
15. Drift, drift, what to lean on?
16. Abrupt death! yet reappear.
17. Blown over the Eight Lakes,
18. Driven up the Five Mountains,
19. Flow and tumble, no constant place.
20. Who knows my distress?
21. I'd rather be grass in the woods
22. To get burnt with autumn
23. Not that destruction is no pain
24. But that I want to be with root.

陶潛

挽歌詩

荒草何茫茫
白楊亦蕭蕭
嚴霜九月中
送我出遠郊
四面無人居
高墳正嶕嶢
馬為仰天鳴
風為自蕭條
幽室一已閉
千年不復朝
千年不復朝
賢達無奈何
向來相送人
各自還其家
親戚或餘悲
他人亦已歌
死去何所道
託體同山阿

1. wild	grass	how	vast broad	vast broad
2. white	poplar/s	also	*hsiao* (onomatopoeic)	*hsiao*
3. harsh	frost	ninth	month	middle
4. send	me	off	distant	suburb
5. four	sides	no	man	live
6. tall	tomb/s	now	towering ply-on-ply	— —
7. horse	thereon	lift (i.e., neigh toward the sky)	sky	neigh
8. wind	thereon	self	bleak	—
9. dark	chamber	once	already	close
10. thousand	year/s	not	again	dawn
11. thousand	year/s	not	again	dawn
12. sage	the-wise	cannot	help	—
13. in-the-past	—	each-other	see-off	people
14. each	self	return	his	home
15. relatives	—	perhaps	remaining	sorrowful
16. other	people	also	already (ie. make merriment)	sing
17. being-death-and-gone		where what	(to)	go
18. entrust	body	to	mountain	bend

1. Wild grass, miles on end.
2. White poplars go sough-sough.
3. Biting frost in late autumn:
4. You see me off to the wastes.
5. All four sides: no man dwells.
6. Tall tombs, ply upon ply.
7. Horses neigh toward the sky.
8. Wind, by itself, blows bleak,
9. Dark chamber once closed,
10. Never will I see dawn again.
11. Never will I see dawn again.
12. Worthies can do nothing.
13. All mourners who came
14. Would return, each his own way.
15. Relatives may still grieve;
16. Others have already sung.
17. Where do the dead go after death?
18. Lodge the body with mountains.

行路難　　鮑照

酒琴帳篏筝沈思吟上音
美雕羽錦將歌減路催吹
之之之歲時且行銅清
厄匣荃菌落轉悲節梁時
金玉芙蒲零宛裁抵柏古
君媚彩華顏光君我見鬧
奉壽七九紅寒願聽不宇

FROM *WEARY ROAD: 18 SONGS*

NO. 1   *Pao Chao (421–465)*

1. serve	you	gold	cup	's	beautiful	wine
2. tortoise	—	jade	chest case	's	carved	lute
3. seven	color	hibiscus	—	's	feather	net
4. nine	flower	grape	—	's	brocade	quilt
5. red	face	wither	fall	year	about-to	dusk
6. cold	light	smoothly	turn	time	about-to	sink
7. wish	you	cut-off	sorrow	and	reduce	thinking
8. listen-to	me	beat	*chieh* (a musical instrument used to beat the time)	walk	road (i.e., the tune of "Weary Road")	chant
9. not	see	Cypress	Beams	Brazen	Bird	on
10. rather	hear	old ancient	times	clear	pipe	tune

1. To you, fine wine in gold cup,
2. Carved lute in jade and shell case,
3. Feather-curtains of seven-colored hibiscus,
4. Brocade quilt of nine-flowered vines.
5. Rosy cheeks fade: dusk closes in.
6. Cold light revolves, about to sink.
7. Please cut your sorrows, thin your thoughts
8. And listen to my beat to the "Weary Road"
9. Do you not see the Terraces of Cypress Beam and Brazen Bird?*
10. How now to hear the clear notes of those ancient flutes?

* Both Terraces (Cypress Beam built by Emperor Wu of Han, Brazen Bird by Ts'ao Ts'ao of Wei) were places of luxurious feasting and extravagant music.

瀉水置平地
各自東西南北流
人生亦有命
安能行歎復坐愁
酌酒以自寬
舉杯斷絶歌路難
心非木石豈無感
吞聲躑躅不敢言

1.	splash	water	put place	level	ground		
2.	each	self	east	west	south	north	flow
3.	man's	life	also	has	destiny		
4.	how	can	walk	sigh	and	sit	grieve
5.	pour	wine	to	self	console		
6.	raise	cup	break-off	sing	road (i.e., "Weary Road")	difficult	
7.	heart	not	wood	stone	how	no	feeling
8.	swallow	sound	hesitate	—	not	dare	speak

1. Splash water on level ground.
2. Water flows by itself east, west, south, north.
3. Life has its own track.
4. Why walk sighing, sit grieving?
5. Drink, drink to free yourself
6. Toast and cut off sorrow and sing "Weary Road"
7. Heart is not born stone, no, not insensible,
8. I only swallow my sobs, hesitate and dare not say.

草滿道
邊春上去出當入歡在數沽非付
河死城沒復何永苦敷得恒竹貴
見枯見沒復何永去生氣願頭名亡
不時不暝朝我去生氣願頭名存
君冬君今明今一人意且枕功存

得黃樂盛相酒我皇
然泉少年就錢事天

NO. 5

1.	you	not
2.	winter	time
3.	you	not
4.	this	evening
5.	tomorrow	morning
6.	now	I
7.	once	go
8.	man's	life
9.	aspirations	—
10.	(part.)	wish
11.	bed	head
12.	rank	fame
13.	life	death

see	river	side	grass	
wither	die	spring	fill	road (?)
see	wall	above	sun	
disappear	completely	off		
anew	appear (?)			
what	time	should	achieve	(part.)
eternally	perish	enter	yellow	spring
bitterness	more	joy	—	less
widespread	fertile	in	prosperous	year
get	what-one-wills	repeatedly	to-each-other	accommodate
forever	there-is	buy	wine	money
bamboo	silk	not	my	business
(i.e., historical records)				
distinction	obscurity humbleness	entrust	emperor	heaven

1. Do you not see the riverside grass
2. Withers in winter, grows a full road in spring?
3. Do you not see the sun above the wall
4. Sinks to nothing this evening
5. Emerges anew tomorrow?
6. When can I attain what I ought?
7. Once gone; external extinction into the Yellow Springs.
8. In life, much suffering, little joy
9. Full swing of energy is in blooming youth
10. To attain ambitions, meet, meet often.
11. At bed-head, always money for wine.
12. Rank and name or bamboo and silk, heck with them.
13. Life, death, high, low, leave them to Heavens.

去
軍還陰靉飛寒何顏
從得夜河雲氣奈留
少離宦斷條急人望胡子世
壯不日阻白邊兮得跡難轊抑起
見流宦斷蕭哀愁遠胡妻生摧
不首鄉塵風笛此山死見兒憂
君白故音朔胡聽登將能男綿

軻 欲 何 道 長 歎

1. you	not
2. white	head
3. old	country (i.e., hometown)
4. sound	dust
5. north	wind
6. Tartar	flute
7. hear	this
8. climb	mountain
9. about-to	die
10. can (To see)	see
11. male	son
12. continuous	sorrow press

see	young	sturdy	join	army	go		
drift	scatter	cannot	—	return			
distant	distant	day	night	separate			
break	cut-off	obstruct block	river	pass			
bleak	—	white	cloud	fly			
sorrowful	abrupt	border	air	cold			
sadden	people	(part.)	what-else-can-be-done				
distantly	look	get	preserve remaining	face			
Tartar	horse	hoof-prints tracks					
wife	—	difficult					
born (in)	world	hardship	——	desire	what	speak	
sad	depressed	rise	long	sigh			
lift							

1. Do you not see the young men off to war,
2. Now white-headed, still drift and drift: no return?
3. Home so distant, cut off day and night.
4. Voices, activities, all blocked by rivers and passes.
5. North wind blows bleak: White clouds fly.
6. Tartar flutes, shrill and sharp; border air, biting cold.
7. This music grieves men, Ai! what to do?
8. Climb mountains. Look afar. To catch their parting youth!
9. Death it will be under Tartar hoofs
10. To see their wives, how hard!
11. Men born to this world: rugged life! what to say?
12. Endless sorrow rending heart, they rise to sigh.

FROM THE *YÜEH-FU*

OF THE SOUTHERN DYNASTIES

FOUR "TZU-YEH" SONGS

NO. I

1.	setting	sun	come-out-of emerge-from	door	front
2.	watch	—	see	you	pass
3.	charming	face	plenty-of	beautiful	continuations-of-the hairline-in-front-the ears
4.	fragrance	—	already	fill	road

1. At sunset I come out of the door
2. And watch you walk past.
3. Fine makeup, charm-filled locks:
4. Fragrance already a full street.

芳是香所為
冶容不敢當
天不奪人顧
故使儂見郎

NO. 2

1.	fragrance	is	perfume	what	does
	(i.e., fragrance is due to the perfume)				
2.	charming	face	not	dare	deserve
3.	heaven	not	deprive	man's	desire
4.	so	make	me	see	you

1. Fragrance is due to perfumes
2. Fine makeup is overpraise.
3. Heaven tampers not my wish
4. And so makes me see you.

頭肩上憐
梳兩膝可
不被兩不
昔髮伸處
宿絲婉何

NO. 3

1. last-night   —   not   comb   head (i.e., hair)
2. silk   hair   cover   two   shoulders
3. curl   sprawl   your   knees lap   on
4. which   place   not   lovely

1. Last night with hair unbrushed:
2. Silks of black over two shoulders
3. Curled up on your knees,
4. Which part is not lovely?

夜長不得眠
明月何灼灼
想聞散喚聲
虛應空中諾

NO. 4

1.	night	long	cannot	—	sleep
2.	bright clear	moon	how	bright (gleaming bright)	bright
3.	think	hear	scattered	calling	voice
4.	vainly	respond	sky (i.e., the air)	midst	yes

1. Long night: unable to sleep
2. The moon, how breakingly bright.
3. Calling, someone seems calling.
4. Into the empty air, I answer "Yes?"

于夜四時歌（春歌）

春春春吹　林鳥風我　花意復羅　多多多裳　媚哀情開

SPRING SONG FROM "TZU-YEH" SONGS
OF THE FOUR SEASONS

1. spring	forest grove	flower	much	charm
2. spring	bird	message meaning	much	moving
3. spring	wind	furthermore	much	sentiment feeling
4. blow	my	silk	dress	open

1. Spring groves: flowers, such charm.
2. Spring birds: calls so in tune.
3. Spring winds full of feeling
4. Lift up the hems of my skirt.

清溪小姑曲

開門白水
側近橋梁
小姑所居
獨處無郎

SONG OF THE LITTLE MISS BY THE GREEN RILL

1. open	door	white	water
2. side	near	bridge	—
3. little	maiden	(where)	live
4. alone	stay	without	mate
			boy

1. Open door: white water.
2. Upon it a bridge is laid.
3. Little miss lives alone
4. Alone without a mate.

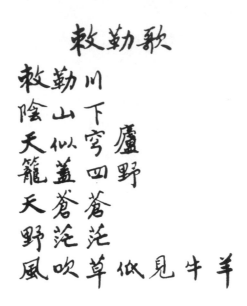

TCHIREK SONG (NORTHERN YÜEH-FU)

1.	Tchirek	—	River				
2.	Shade; Dark	Mountain	below				
3.	heaven	like	arched	tent			
			(i.e., Mongolian tent)				
4.	hover	cover	four	wilderness			
5.	heaven	gray	gray				
6.	wilderness	vast	vast				
		broad	broad				
7.	wind	blow	grass	low	see	cattle	sheep

1. Tchirek River
2. Beneath Dark Mountains.
3. The sky is arched like a tent,
4. Caging steppe's four ends.
5. The sky so gray,
6. Wilderness so vague,
7. The winds blow, the grass leans low and see the cattle go.

LANDSCAPE POETRY

SHAN-SHUI-SHIH **OR POEMS OF**

"MOUNTAINS AND RIVERS"

The rise of landscape poetry (*Shan-sui-shih*, or poems of "Mountains and Rivers") in the third and fourth centuries played a key role in a shift of sensibility that led to the formation of an aesthetic attitude uniquely Chinese. This attitude calls for the poet to release the objects in Phenomenon from their seeming irrelevance and bring forth their original freshness and thingness—return to their first innocence, so to speak—thus, making them relevant as "self-so-complete" objects in their co-extensive existence. This poetry can be achieved by a devoted focus of attention upon the objects as they are and an unequivaocal affirmation and acceptance of them as such. The poet's job is to approximate the cuts and turns of our immediate perceiving contact with the objects in their original condition.

The beginning and growth of this imaginative dimension has a history too vast and too complicated for the present brief introduction. It must be reserved for another occasion. The ancient Chinese had always been delighted in the natural sublimeness of the mountains and rivers; they were referred to as "beautifully alive," harboring sacredness and demanding reverence; they were compared to kind and wise men. But in almost all ancient Chinese poems, such as those in *Shih Ching* and *Ch'u Tz'u*, landscape remained as a backdrop against which human events took place. Its emergence from this subordinate position to a prominent and independent object for aesthetic consideration had to wait until the radical cultural change of the third and fourth centuries. Briefly, this period witnessed the reaction against the dead rigidity and superficiality of the Han codification of the Confucian system, the revival of Taoism, the popularization of Buddhism by way of Taoist interpretations, and large groups of intellectuals seeking affinity with nature by residing in mountains where they could enjoy them in their untrammeled fullness.

The central force in shaping this landscape awareness is the Taoist mental horizon which begins by rejecting the premise that the structure of Phenomenon is the same as we conceive it. All conscious efforts in ordering it will result in superficial structures imposed upon undifferentiated existence and hence distorting it. It asks us to view things as things view themselves, to lose ourselves into Phenomenon, into the flux of events, the million changes constantly happening before us. As Kuo Hsiang (d. 312), commenting on Chuang Tzu's concept of change, put it:

> The sage roams in the path of a million changes—a million things, a million changes—and thus, he changes in accordance with the law of a million changes.

Since Tao (the Way) is the totality of all things as they are and is not something transcending the world of beings, (this view was particularly popular after Kuo Hsiang's commentary in which he explicitly did away with the view of a creator; see also Hsieh Ling-yün's poems in this selection), mountains and rivers, as recluse-intellectuals put it, are themselves Tao. They, like other forms of beings in Phenomenon, are right and adequate and complete in and by themselves and need no human justification (such as naming, imparting meaning, and ordering) for being such.

This view, from another angle, could be labeled as antispeech and anti-art. A poet must mediate between Phenomenon, which has its complete "self-so" existence, and language, which is a human-conceived intellectual entity, in order to produce a poem. We almost have to agree with Wordsworth that

> Minds that have nothing to confer
> Find little to perceive.

But the Taoist denunciation of egoist enterprise helps to bring forth a special type of mediation—a mediation that emphasizes continual decrease in discursive, analytical, and explanatory procedures leading toward an art of noninterference (or, to put it more aptly, of the least interference). This is, however, not to say that such a nonmediating mediation was at work from the very beginning. The early Orchid Pavilion poets, for instance, had to mediate by referring back to the Taoist concept of change:

> Before our eyes, Pattern displays itself
> Immense, Transformation!
> A million differences, none out of tune.
> Pipings all variegated:
> What fits me, none strange.

But as we progress from these early landscapists, we find continuous elimination of such unnecessary intellectual justification and, with Wang Wei of the T'ang Dynasty, we have approached almost the purest landscape poem, in which the poet resides his voice in the objects and lets them speak and act themselves out, leaving us the sole witness to the workings of nature.

觀滄海　　曹操

東臨碣石
以觀滄海
水何澹澹
山島竦峙
樹木叢生
百草豐茂
秋風蕭瑟
洪波湧起
日月之行
若出其中
星漢粲爛
若出其裡
幸甚至哉
歌以詠志

VIEW OF THE BLUE SEA *Ts'ao Ts'ao*

1.	eastward	up-to face	monolith (i.e., the mountain by the sea)	stone
2.	to	view	blue	sea
3.	water	how	rolling	rolling
4.	mountain	islet	towering	standing-upright
5.	trees	—	in-clusters	grow
6.	hundred	plant/s	luxuriant	—
7.	autumn	wind/s	*hsiao* (onomatopoeic)	*se*
8.	big	wave/s	surge	up
9.	sun	moon	's	trek journey
10.	seem	emerge-from	its	midst
11.	Milky-Way	—	glitter	—
12.	seem	emerge-from	its	inside
13.	luck	quite	come	(part.)
14.	sing	to	express	will feeling

1. Eastward, overlooking the Monolith:
2. To view the blue sea.
3. How rolling, the water!
4. Sky-piercing, mountain isles.
5. Trees vie in growth.
6. Grasses so profuse.
7. Autumn winds sough
8. Big waves swell up.
9. Sun and moon's trek
10. Seems to come out of it.
11. Milky Way's explosive brightness
12. Seems to come out from there.
13. [An occasion fit
14. To sing a song to it.]

POEMS FROM THE *ORCHID*

PAVILION COLLECTION

Wang Hsi-chih (321–379)

PREFACE (IN PART)

In the ninth year of Yung-ho (353), the year of Kuei-ch'ou, in the last weeks of spring (the third day of the third month), we gathered in the Orchid Pavilion near Shan-yin of Kuei-ch'i: it was Purification Festival. Talented men, young and old, came. Here, lofty mountains and handsome peaks, thick forests and tall bamboos. Next, clear streams, rushing torrents. Like belts, they reflected both sides. With these, floating goblets on meandering waters. We sat down in line. Although we did not have strings and pipes, we drank and chanted, enough to fully pour out our feelings. That day, bright sun and clear air. Winds are tuneful. We looked up: immense, the universe! We looked down, so full, things and things! Therefore, let the eyes go on an excursion, let the bosom gallop, enough to exhaust the pleasure of sight and hearing. Truly a joy, this occasion! . . .

蘭亭　　　　王羲之

仰視碧天際
俯瞰淥水濱
寥闃無涯觀
寓目理自陳
大矣造化工
萬殊莫不均
群籟雖參差
適我無非新

ORCHID PAVILION *Wang Hsi-chih*

1. upward	look	blue	sky	end
2. downward	look	green	water	brink
3. empty lonely	silent	no	end	watch
4. rely (i.e., gaze, look closely)	eye	pattern	by-itself	present manifest display
5. magnificent	(part.)	creation	Transformation (i.e., creative and governing forces in nature)	work
6. ten-thousand differences		none	not	equal in-equilibrium
7. various	pipe	though	long-and-short	—
8. suit	me	none	not	new

1. Looking up: blue sky's end.
2. Looking down: green water's brim.
3. Deep solitude: rimless view.
4. Before the eyes, a Pattern displays itself.
5. Immense, Transformation!
6. A million differences, none out of tune.
7. Pipings all variegated:
8. What fits me, none strange.

蘭亭　孫綽

渚㿸竹濤藻戢甘韶
枉九脩瀾雲纖不聞
拂蔭吟戲落剚豈在
風雲語鱗筆言珍味
流停鶯游携微時忘

ORCHID PAVILION   *Sun Ch'o (320?–380?)*

1.	flowing	wind/s	flap brush	Meandering (i.e., a place name)	Islet
2.	pausing	cloud/s	shade	nine (i.e., nine-rimmed)	lake/s
3.	oriole/s	language	chant	slender	bamboo/s
4.	swimming	scales (i.e., fish)	sport	surging	wave/s
5.	carry	brush	fall (i.e., capture)	cloud	pattern
6.	subtle	word	dissect	thin (the minute)	hair
7.	timely	treasure (i.e., rare dishes in season)	how	not	delicious
8.	forget	taste	in	hearing	Shao (i.e., presumably Emperor Shun's music)

1. Flowing winds brush Meandering Islet.
2. Gathering clouds shade deep lakes.
3. Orioles sing among tall bamboos.
4. Swimming fishes sport with surging waves.
5. With a pen—to pluck foliage of clouds.
6. Abstruse words—to bare the minute.
7. Not that rare dishes are not sweet
8. Oblivious of taste in the music of Shao.

蘭亭　　王彬之

鮮葩映林薄
游鱗戲清渠
臨川欣投釣
得意豈在魚

ORCHID PAVILION　*Wang Pin-Chih (fl. 400)*

1.	fresh	flower	shine	forest —
				sward —
2.	sporting	scales	play	clear stream
3.	at facing	stream	happily	cast fishing-hook
4.	get (i.e., feel at home)	satisfaction heart's content	how-could-it-be	in fish

1. Beaming flowers in the thicket
2. Sporting fishes in clear stream.
3. At the bank, cast a line—
4. Fully content—fish or no fish.

三月三日臨曲水　庾闡

THE 3RD DAY OF THE 3RD MONTH AT
THE MEANDERING RIVER *Yü Ch'an (c. 286–339)*

1.	dusk	spring	wash	clear	brimming-water
2.	sporting	scales (fish)	swim	one	gorge
3.	tall	fountain	spurt	east	small-but-tall-peak
4.	surging	big-wave/s	from	clean	fountain
5.	at; facing	stream	repeated	curve	flow
6.	luxuriant thick	forest	shine	green	sward
7.	light	boat	sink	floating	goblet
8.	drum (v.)	oar	watch	fish	jump frisk

1. Spring's end: washing in clear water.
2. Sporting fishes swim a full gorge.
3. A high fountain spurts from East Peak.
4. Rushing waves: such clean gurgling.
5. Overlooking—curves and curves of river.
6. Thick forest glimmers with greensward.
7. Light boats sink flying goblets.
8. Drumming of oars—fish frisk.

帆入南湖　　湛方生

江阜路首流有遠久中後
三眾川嚴時時推長宙先
紀主淨蔚何何互獨宇迷
蟲岳沙松水山運器悠今
彭廬白青此此人茲悠古

SAILING INTO THE SOUTH LAKE   *Chan Fang-sheng (fl. 400)*

1. P'eng (i.e., name of the lake now known as Po-yang Lake)	Li	sum-up join; command	three	rivers
2. Lu	Mountain	master	other all	hills
3. white	sand	clean	river	way course
4. green	pine	make-green	crag	head
5. this	water	what	time	flow
6. this	mountain	what	time	there-is
7. man	destiny	with-each-other	push (i.e., mutate)	move
8. these	media forms	alone	long-lasting	—
9. distant	distant	universe	—	middle
10. antiquity	present	replace	former	latter

1. P'eng-li commands three rivers.
2. Mount Lu masters other hills.
3. White sand cleans the waterway.
4. Green pines cover hanging crags.
5. This water: since when, its flow?
6. This mountain: since when, its being?
7. Man's fate changes from this to that!
8. These forms alone stay forever.
9. Within the distant reach of the cosmos,
10. Past, present, in order, first, last.

高岳萬丈峻
長湖千里清
白沙窮年潔
林松冬夏青
水無暫停流
木有千年貞
寤言載新詩
忽忘羈客情

還都帆　　湛方生

SAILING BACK TO THE CAPITAL　*Chan Fang-sheng*

1.	high	range	ten-thousand	ten-Chinese feet	high
2.	long	lake	thousand	mile/s	clear
3.	white	sand	exhaust	year	clean
4.	forest	pine/s	winter	summer	green
5.	water	no	temporarily	stop	flowing
6.	wood	has	thousand	year/s	constancy
7.	wake	say (part.)	compose	new	poem
8.	suddenly	forget	detained	guest alien	feeling

1. High mountains, a million feet, skyward.
2. Long lakes, a thousand miles, clear.
3. White sand, all year long, clean.
4. Pine-groves, winter or summer, green.
5. Water never for a second stops flowing.
6. Trees, for a thousand years, firm.
7. Waking: to write new poems;
8. All of a sudden, gone, a traveler's sadness.

遊仙詩　　　郭璞

翡翠戲蘭色蘿更高籠相一茗鮮林山士絃外泉遊煙袖肩輩年
容綠蒙籠有冥撫凌寂清霄飛上紫丘崖蝴鶴
中靜放嚼結蓋有嘯情抱臨乘浮洪蜉龜
赤駕左右借宵藥松鴻把柑問知

FROM *POEMS ON ROAMING WITH IMMORTALS* *Kuo P'u (276–324)*

1. Kingfishers sport among orchids and begonias,
2. Color to color, sheen flashes upon sheen.
3. Green vines braid into the high forest
4. Thick foliage roofs a whole mountain.
5. Beneath these a lone meditative man
6. Silently whistles, plucking at the clear strings.
7. He lets loose his heart through the sky,
8. Chews pistils and bails out flying fountains.
9. The "Red Pine" stands before the up-stream,*
10. Riding a wild-goose upon the purple smoke.
11. He takes "Floating Hill" by the sleeve
12. And pats the "Vast Cliff" upon the shoulder.
13. You, you ephemeras
14. Would you rather know the age of a turtle?

*Red Pine, Floating Hill, Vast Cliff are the names of three famous Taoist recluses.
The names themselves show the stress of the Taoist desire to become consonant with Nature.

於南山往北山經湖中瞻眺

謝靈運

朝旦發陽崖，景落憩陰峯。
舍舟眺迥渚，停策倚茂松。
側逕既窈窕，環洲亦玲瓏。
俛視喬木杪，仰聆大壑淙。
石橫水分流，林密蹊絕蹤。
解作竟何感，升長皆豐容。
初篁苞綠籜，新蒲含紫茸。
海鷗戲春岸，天雞弄和風。
撫化心無厭，覽物眷彌重。
不惜去人遠，但恨莫與同。
孤遊非情歎，賞廢理誰通。

SCENE FROM SOUTH HILL TO NORTH HILL PASSING THE LAKE . . . * *Hsieh Ling-yün (385–433)*

1. Dawn: off from the south cliff.
2. Sundown: rest on the north peak.
3. Boat left ashore, to pore into distant islands.
4. Staff laid aside, to lean on a thick pine.
5. Sidepaths lean and long.
6. Round islets bright and clear.
7. Looking down: tips of tall trees.
8. Harkening above: water rushes from large valleys.
9. A crisscross rock splits the stream.
10. A dense forest blocks all paths.
11. Sky thaws: thundering rains: how about them?[1]
12. Vegetation rises up in profusion.
13. First bamboo-shoots wrapped in green sheaths.
14. New reeds hold purple fluffs.
15. Seagulls sport on spring shores.
16. Pheasants play in mild winds.
17. Cherish Transformation: mind will be unbound. [2]
18. Embrace things: love will deepen.
19. One need not regret that men of past are distant.
20. Sad it is to find no one of like mind.
21. To roam alone is not emotional relief:
22. Appreciation now abandoned—cosmic scheme: who knows?

*The present translation follows Yeh Hsiao-hsueh's excellent annotations (see *Hsieh Ling-yün shih-hsuan*, p. 90).

1. The reference is to *The Book of Changes (I Ching)*, Ch. 40., which runs, in the hands of Wilhelm/Baynes, "When heaven and earth deliver themselves, thunder and rain set in. When thunder and rain set in, the seed pods of all fruits, plants and trees break open." Hsieh extracted only two words from this reference, i.e., Deliver/set-in, to infer this concept. Mine is a poetic improvisation.
2. Transformation refers to the concept of change expounded in Chuang Tzu's "The Great and Venerable Teacher." Kuo Hsiang's commentary is particularly relevant: "The sage roams in the path of a million changes—a million things, a million changes—and thus, he changes in accordance with the law of a million changes."

從斤竹澗越嶺溪行　謝靈運

猿鳴誠知曙，谷幽光未顯。
巖下雲方合，花上露猶泫。
逶迤傍隈隩，迢遞陟陘峴。
過澗既厲急，登棧亦陵緬。
川渚屢逕復，乘流翫迴轉。
蘋萍泛沈深，菰蒲冒清淺。
企石挹飛泉，攀林摘葉卷。
想見山阿人，薜蘿若在眼。
握蘭勤徒結，折麻心莫展。
情用賞為美，事昧竟誰辨。
觀此遺物慮，一悟得所遣。

FROM CHIN-CHU CREEK, PAST THE RIDGE, ALONG THE STREAM ... *Hsieh Ling-yün*

1. monkey/s	cry	really	know	dawn
2. valley/s	obscure	light	not-yet	show
3. crag/s	below	cloud/s	just	close
4. flower/s	on	dew	still	about-to-drip
5. long continuous	— —	skirt (v.) leaning-against	curved	mountain-side
6. distant	—	hike pass	sloping	small-but-tall-mountain
7. pass	creek	(not-only)	wade	torrent
8. ascend	plank-path	(also)	travel-beyond	the-remote
9. river	islet	repeatedly	go walk	return
10. ride	stream	play	whirl	turn
11. duckweed/s	—	float	sunken (i.e., great)	depth
12. Hydropyrum	Latifolia	stick-out-of cover	clear	shallow
13. tiptoe	stone	gather-with-a-vessel	flying	fountain
14. climb	forest	pluck	leave/s	curl
15. think desire	see	mountain	—	man
16. fig-leaves	mistletoe	as-if	in	eye
17. hold	orchid/s	industriously	in-vain	tie
18. break	hemp	heart	not	expand
19. feeling	use	delight	as	beauty
20. thing	obscure	even	who	distinguish
21. watch	this	lose	material (worldly)	worry
22. one	awareness	get	what	give-up

1. Monkeys cry: dawn, they know.
2. Valleys still dark: no light visible.
3. Beneath the peak, clouds close up.
4. On the flowers, dews drip.
5. Twisting, turning—along mountain bends,
6. Up among far reaching braes,
7. Past the creek, trailing across torrents,
8. Ascend plank-paths, into the distance.
9. River, islets thrown out and winding back.
10. Ride the current, enjoy the many turns.
11. Duckweeds float on dark deeps.
12. Reeds, rushes cover clear shallows.
13. Tiptoe on rocks to catch a cup of flying spring:
14. Tug the trees to pluck budding leaves.
15. There looms this Man of the Mountains,
16. Full-clad in fig leaves and mistletoe,
17. Holding orchids vainly waiting for friendship:
18. Plucking hemps: no way to bare his heart.
19. What one feels becomes beauty—
20. This subtle truth: who would share?
21. To view thus releases worries of the world.
22. A flash of awakening: everything is dispelled.

夜發石關亭　謝靈運

隨山踰千里
浮溪將十夕
鳥歸息舟楫
星闌命行役
亭亭曉月暎
泠泠朝露滴

NIGHT: SETTING OUT FROM SHIH-KUAN PAVILION

Hsieh ling-yün

1. follow	mountain/s	exceed	thousand	mile/s
2. drift	stream	almost	ten	evening/s
3. bird/s	return	rest	boat	oar
4. star/s	become-scarce	order	go-on-a-mission (weary trip)	
5. brightly	—	morning	moon	shine
6. cold	—	morning	dew	drop

1. Followed mountains over a thousand miles,
2. Floated on a stream for almost ten evenings.
3. Birds return: boats and oars put aside.
4. Stars thinned out: a long weary trip.
5. High and bright, morning moon.
6. Cold, so cold, early dewdrips.

登廬山　　鮑照

懸裝亂水區，薄旅次山楩。
千巖盛阻積，萬登勢迴蒙。
籠從高昔籠，紛亂襲前名。
洞澗窺地脈，簞樹隱天經。
松磴上迷密，雲寶下微橫。
陰冰寶夏結，炎樹信冬榮。
嘈嘴晨鼯思，叫蕭夜猿清。
深崖伏化迹，穹岫閟長靈。
乘此樂山性，重以遠遊情。
方蹤羽人逡，永與煙霧并。

ASCEND LU-SHAN *Pao Chao*

1. Hanging lugguage disturbs shadows in the water.
2. Our trip ends in a mountain house.
3. Blocking, piling up, a thousand cliffs rise.
4. Twisting, turning, descend a million valleys,
5. Imposing as antiquity itself.
6. Profuse, confused, one assumes the other's name.
7. From deep torrents, earth's veins can be seen.
8. Among spearing trees, sky's network is hidden.
9. Stone bridges reach into dense mist.
10. Cloud-caves pour down the four directions.
11. Sombre ice is frozen in summer.
12. Flaming trees flourish in winter.
13. In the morning, the clamor of jungle-fowls.
14. At night, clear cries of monkeys.
15. Among steep precipices, traces of Transformation.
16. Upon the peaks, the lasting spirit.
17. To follow this delight in mountains' natures
18. And deep love for long excursions
19. We will mount upon the road of feathered men
20. And merge forever with smoke and mist.

之宣城出新林浦向板橋　謝朓

江路西南永，歸流東北騖。
天際識歸舟，雲中辨江樹。
旅思倦搖搖，孤遊昔已屢。
既歡懷祿情，復協滄洲趣。
囂塵自茲隔，賞心於此遇。
雖無玄豹姿，終隱南山霧。

TO HSÜAN-CH'ENG, PAST HSIN-LIN-P'U, TOWARD
PAN-CH'IAO *Hsieh T'iao (464–499)*

1.	river	way	southwest	—	extend
2.	return	flow	northeast	—	speed
3.	sky's	end	know	returning	boat
4.	cloud	middle	distinguish	smoke	tree
5.	traveling	thought	tired	slowly rolling	slowly rolling
6.	lone	travel	formerly	already	repeat
7.	(both)	delight	harbor	official-distinction rank	feeling
8.	(and)	agree	blue (i.e., hermit's land)	cove	interest
9.	noisy worldly	dust	from	now	separate
10.	delight	heart	at	this	unexpected encounter
11.	though	without	black	leopard	build posture
12.	finally	become-a-recluse retreat	South	Hill	mist

1. Endless, waterway toward the southwest,
2. Rushing flux—this trip toward the northeast,
3. Sky's end: mark a returning boat.
4. Among clouds: smoke or trees?
5. A tired traveler's thoughts, rolling, rolling.
6. Alone on the road: numerous times.
7. Already spent with the pleasures of office,
8. Now in tune with the joys of Blue Coves
9. Stirring dust now gone,
10. Meet the heart's wish here.
11. No Black Leopard's build—
12. Yet a recluse in the mist of South Hill.

晚登三山還望京邑　謝朓

灞涘望長安　河陽視京縣
白日麗飛甍　參差皆可見
餘霞散成綺　澄江靜如練
喧鳥覆春洲　雜英滿芳甸
去矣方滯淫　懷哉罷歡宴
佳期悵何許　淚下如流霰
有情知望鄉　誰能鬒不變

ASCEND THE THREE MOUNTAINS TOWARD THE EVENING: LOOKING BACK AT THE CAPITAL *Hsieh T'iao*

#				
1. Pa (-ling)	riverside	watch	Ch'ang	An district
2. Ho	Yang	view	Capital	district
3. white	sun	shine; light-up	flying	beams eaves
4. long-and-short	—	all	can (i.e., visible)	see
5. remaining	twilight clouds	scatter	become	brocade
6. transparent	river	quite	like	silk
7. clamorous	bird/s	cover	spring	islet/s
8. mixed	flower/s	fill	fragrant	field
9. go	(part.)	then	inert	long
10. miss	(part.)	forsake	cheerful	banquet
11. good	date	feel-at-a-loss	how	much
12. tears	down	like	flowing	hail sleet
13. have there-is	feeling	know	watch	home-land
14. who	can	black-hair	not	change

1. From Pa-ling, the sight of Ch'ang-an.
2. From Ho-yang, the view of the Capital.
3. The white glare lights up flights of eaves,
4. Long and short edges, all visible.
5. Last clouds scatter into brocade.
6. The transparent river is quiet like silk.
7. Clamors of birds overwhelm the spring isle.
8. Mixed flowers fill the fragrant field.
9. Go. Go. Why stay here so long?
10. To be home! Stop the merriment here.
11. When, a date to return?
12. Tear: shed like spattering sleet.
13. Who, stirred with longing for home,
14. Can keep his black hair from changing?

遊東田　　　謝　朓

戚戚苦無悰，携手共行樂。
尋雲陟層榭檻，隨山闇藹漠。
遠樹藹新亦落，煙餘酒動戲芳青郭。
對春青。

魚山戲荷花春山，鳥不還。

ROAMING THE EAST FIELD *Hsieh T'iao*

1. sorrowful	sorrowful	suffer-from	no	pleasure
2. take	hand	together	practice	pleasure
(i.e., hand in hand)			(i.e., enjoy oneself)	
3. seek	cloud/s	hike	serried laddered	terrace-with-trees
4. follow	mountain/s	watch	mushroom	tower
5. distant	tree/s	misty obscure	thriving	—
6. growing uprising	smoke	profusely	file-over-file lined-up	—
7. fish	sport	new	lotus-leaves	stir
8. bird/s	scatter	remaining	flower/s	drop fall
9. not	face	fragrant	spring	wine
10. still	watch	green	mountain	outline wall

1. Smitten with sorrow, overcast with gloom
2. Hold hands to go out for fun.
3. To search for clouds, up serried terrace,
4. Along mountains to view the mushroom towers.
5. Distant trees, misty, file over file.
6. Growing smoke, drifting, silk weaving silk.
7. Fishes sport: new lotus-leaves stir.
8. Birds scatter: last flowers fall.
9. No more flower-spring-drinking,
10. Look toward green mountain walls.

望 三 湖　　　謝 朓

霞翼近直秀色人榱
頹歸遠紆春秋栽何
照望周見向共傷復
水臺原汀難黃暮媛
積高平連葳芸薄嬋

VIEWING THE THREE LAKES　*Hsieh T'iao*

1. accumulated confluent	water	reflect	red	cloud/s
2. high	terrace	watch	return	feather (i.e., birds)
3. plain/s	—	encircle	far	near
4. stretching connected	shore/s river-islet/s	show	curved	straight
5. luxuriant	—	toward	spring	grow
6. extreme	yellow	share	autumn	color
7. dusk	—	feel-sad	(part.)	man
8. interwoven involved committed	— — —	again	where	end

1. Confluent water mirror red clouds.
2. High terrace to view returning birds;
3. Plains, all around, far and near.
4. Connected islets, meandering and straight.
5. Luxuriance—growth of spring.
6. Fading yellow shares autumn's tone.
7. Dusk: sadness over friends,
8. So interwoven, when to end?

江皋曲　　王融

林斷山更續
洲盡江復開
雲峰帝鄉起
水源桐柏来

THE RIVER SONG *Wang Yung (468–485)*

1.	forest/s	break	mountain/s	further again	continue
2.	islet/s	finish	river	again	open
3.	cloud	peak/s	emperor (i.e., god's residence; king's native place; capital)	village/s	rise
4.	water	source	sycamore/s	cedar/s	come

1. Forests break off. Mountains stretch on still.
2. Islands end. The river opens wide again.
3. From clouded peaks, celestial village emerge.
4. Source of the stream: sycamores and cedars.

遊太平山　　孔稚珪

石　險　天　貌　分
林　交　日　容　缺
陰　澗　落　春　榮
寒　巖　留　夏　雪

TRIP ON MOUNT T'AI-P'ING　*K'ung Chih-kuei (448–501)*

1.	rock/s	steep	heaven	face	separate
2.	forest/s	cross	sun	look	become-incomplete
3.	shadowy	creek	fall	spring	flower/s
4.	cold	crag/s	remain	summer	snow

1. Rocks spear upward: sky's face split.
2. Forests weave: sun's countenance torn
3. Shadowy stream: on it, spring blossoms fall.
4. Cold crags: on them, summer snow.

山 中 雜 詩　　　吳 均

山 際 見 來 煙
竹 中 窺 落 日
鳥 向 簷 上 飛
雲 從 窗 裡 出

FROM MISCELLANEOUS POEMS OF THE MOUNTAINS
Wu Yun (469–520)

1. mountain	end	see	coming	smoke
2. bamboo/s	midst	view	setting	sun
3. bird/s	toward	eaves	upon	fly
4. cloud/s	from	window	inside	come-out

1. From the mountain's end, sight of coming smoke.
2. Through bamboos, the glow of sundown.
3. Birds fly toward the eaves.
4. Clouds come out of the window.

For continuation of this genre, see many examples of Chin-ti-shih in the T'ang Dynasty, especially those of Wang Wei in the pages that follow.

T'IEN-YUAN-SHIH

POEMS OF "FIELDS AND GARDENS"

EXAMPLES FROM T'AO CH'IEN

(365–427)

陶潛

歸園田居

少無適俗韻　性本愛丘山
誤落塵網中　一去三十年
羈鳥戀舊林　池魚思故淵
開荒南野際　守拙歸園田
方宅十餘畝　草屋八九間
榆柳蔭後簷　桃李羅堂前
曖曖遠人村　依依墟里煙
狗吠深巷中　雞鳴桑樹顛
戶庭無塵雜　虛室有餘閒
久在樊籠裡　復得返自然

1. young	no	suit	crowd	temperament
	have-not	fitting	custom	rhythm
2. nature	originally	love	hill/s	mountain/s
instinct				
3. by-mistake	fall-into	dust	net	midst
4. once	go	thirty	—	years
5. detained	bird/s	love	old	forest
6. pooled	fish	miss	old	waters
7. open	the un-	south	wilderness	edge
(till the waste)	cultivated			
8. keep-to	simplicity	return	garden	farm
	coarseness			
9. surrounding	house	ten	odd	acres
10. thatch	house	eight	nine	(unit of mea-
				surement)
11. elm/s	willow/s	shade	back	eaves
12. peach	plum	line	hall	front
13. vague	vague	distant	people	village
14. slender	slender	deserted	village	smoke
15. dog/s	bark	deep	lane	midst
16. rooster	crow	mulberry	tree	top
17. door	yard	no	dust	mix
(i.e., the house)			worldly	confusion,
				meddling
18. empty	room	there-is	remaining	leisure
19. long	in	cage	—	inside
20. again	get-to	return	nature	—
	able-to			

1. Out of tune with the crowd since young:
2. My instinct: love of mountains
3. Chance mistake: fall into world's net.
4. One fall costs thirty long years.
5. Caged birds miss their home forest.
6. Pooled fish long for the deep.
7. I till the waste on the south side.
8. Still unhewn, I return to my farm.
9. Circling my house, some acres of land.
10. Thatched houses, eight or nine.
11. Elms, willows shade the rear eaves.
12. Peach, plum line out the front hall.
13. Hardly visible, distant villages.
14. Cloud-soft, smoke from hamlets.
15. Dogs bark in deep lanes.
16. Cocks crow above mulberries.
17. My house: not a speck of dust.
18. Empty rooms: much quiet leisure.
19. Too long in the shut cage.
20. Now given to return to nature.

其五

還曲淺足酒局闇燭短旭
笫榛且吾熟近中明夕天
獨歷清灌新招室代苦至
恨嶇澗以我雜入薪來復
悵崎山可溉隻日荆歡已

1. disappointed	distressed	lone	cane	return
2. rugged	—	pass	bushes	curve
3. mountain	stream	clear	and	shallow
4. can	—	wash	my	feet
5. strain	my	newly	ripe	wine
6. one	chicken	invite	neighbors	—
7. sun	enter	room	midst	dim
8. bramble	firewood	replace	bright	candle
9. delight	come	bitter (feel sad)	night	short
10. already	again	reach	sky	dawn

1. Distressed: single cane, I return.
2. Rugged road winds through bushes.
3. Mountain stream, shallow and clear,
4. There to wash my feet.
5. Strain a pot of new-brewed wine.
6. Cook a chicken, call the neighbors.
7. Sun verges off: the room darkens.
8. Burn wood for candles.
9. Merriment swells: too short the night!
10. Already the sky whitens with dawn.

飲酒

結廬在人境　而無車馬喧
問君何能爾　心遠地自偏
採菊東籬下　悠然見南山
山氣日夕佳　飛鳥相與還
此中有真意　欲辨已忘言

DRINKING WINE: POEM NO. 5

1. build	house	in	man	region
2. and but	no	carriage/s	horse/s	noise/s
3. ask	you	how	can-be	(part.)
4. mind	distant	place	naturally	incline secluded
5. pick	chrysanthemum/s	east	fence	beneath
6. yu-jan*		catch-sight-of	South	Mountain
7. mountain	air	day (3 or 4 P.M. to dusk)	night	good
8. flying	bird	each-other	with	return
9. this	within	there-is	true	sense-of-things
10. wish	tell	already	forget	word/s

1. A house built within men's reach
2. And no clamor of carts and horses.
3. How, may I ask, can this be?
4. Mind distanced, place becomes remote.
5. Plucking chrysanthemums by the east hedge.
6. I so catch sight of the South Mountain.
7. Mountain so gorgeous in the dusk,
8. Flying birds return wing to wing.
9. Here contains the truth of truth.
10. To tell? Already words are forgotten.

* Literally, distantly, but suggests an unprepared, nondeliberate spontaneous act that follows.

CHIN-T'I-SHIH

POEMS OF NEW METRICAL

PATTERNS

CHIN-T'I-SHIH (LÜ-SHIH,

CHÜEH-CHÜ); KU-SHIH

Chin-t'i-shih is the classification of those poems written according to certain strict metrical rules, dominantly practiced by T'ang and Sung poets in contrast to *Ku-shih* of pre-T'ang poets (as well as those modeled after it) in which such rigid observance is not called for. Specifically, it refers to the following four forms: *wu-lü* (five-character eight-line regulated poems), *ch'i-lü* (seven-character eight-line regulated poems), *wu-chüeh* (five-character four-line "curtailed" poems), and *ch'i-chüeh* (seven-character four-line "curtailed" poems), all of which demand some use of parallelism and fixed tonal positionings (see chart at the end of this introduction).

Although, traditionally, these forms were believed to have been introduced by two early T'ang poets, Shen Ch'uan-ch'i (d. 714) and Sung Chih-wen (d. 712), many pre-T'ang poets such as Hsieh T'iao (464–499), Shen Yo (441–513), Hsü Ling (507–583), Yü Hsin (513–581), and their contemporaries had produced strict regulated poems. The short four-line poems of the Southern *Yüeh-fu* (see Southern *Yüeh-fu*) and similar short poems written by these poets have been rightly claimed as antecedents of the *chüeh-chü* ("curtailed" poems). In fact, it was Shen Yo's formalization of the current theory of discriminating use of the four tones of Chinese characters and the avoidance of what he called "eight-don'ts" which furnished the foundation of the regulated poems. The Chinese characters can be distinguished by four tones or pitches, *level, rising, falling,* and *entering*—the pitch and quantity of the *level* tone being distinctively different from the rest. Thus, the classification of *level* tones is in contrast with *deflected* tones. In choosing words to form a line, a poet, with some deliberation, can select them according to their tonal character and place them in certain alternate positions so that a definite musicality can be achieved (see chart following). The "eight-don'ts" are very restrictive. The first four "don'ts" have to do with avoidance of echoing of tones in certain definite positions (these have direct bearing on metrical rules). To give just one example, "In *wu-lü*, the first character of the first line and the second line must not have the same tone." The other four "don'ts" have to do with avoidance of echoing of rhymes within the lines. Again, one example will suffice: "If the poem should use *hsin* as its rhyming scheme (which usually falls at the end of the second line), no character rhyming with *hsin* would be allowed in all previous nine characters." From these rules were born the sophisticated metrical forms of *lü-shih* and *chüeh-chü* (cut half of the metrical scheme of lü-shih, hence the term "curtailed" poems).

Few poets adhere to these rigid demands in the distribution of tones and rhymes. But most of the T'ang poets took the challenge and some early T'ang poets such as Tu Shen-yen went so far as to ensure no repetitions of tones within all the *deflected* positions. The first two lines of "Harmonizing a Spring Poem by Premier Lu of Chin-ling," for instance, have the following rigid scheme (D = deflected tone; L = level tone; numbers = the three deflected tones: 2 being *rising*, 3, *falling*, and 4, *entering*):

$$
\begin{array}{ccccc}
D4 & D2 & D3 & L & L \\
L & L & D4 & D3 & L
\end{array}
$$

This formalistic sophistication became a huge challenge to the poets who sought to approximate the cuts and turns of the fluctuation of Phenomenon. It belies the basic tenets of the Taoist demand for noninterference. Adherence to the grammar of language (particularly the rhetoric prescribed by Shen Yo) is necessarily superficial. The grammar of language must coincide with the grammar of experience in order to establish authentication for our perceiving act. Here lies the great art of the T'ang poets. Li Po defied the rules and excelled in *Ku-shih*. Wang Wei's poems, more often than not, preserved only tangential observance of these rules and became supreme examples of concrete presentation in his landscape poetry. Tu Fu effected a synthesis of the two. His were rhetorical parallels of the curves of experience. Both the early and the late T'ang poets had been either too submissive to tonal requirements or too emphatic about surface elaboration of diction.

THE METRICAL FORM OF THE CHIN-T'I-SHIH

(A) Five-character eight-line regulated poem (*lü*):

a) "Deflected start"—so called because the tone of the second character of the first line is deflected.

D/L	D	L/D	L	D/L	r
L	L	D	D	L	r
L/D	L	L	D	D	
D/L	D	D	L	L	r
D/L	D	L	L	D	
L	L	D	D	L	r

L/D	L	L	D	D	
D/L	D	D	L	L	r

Notes: 1. D/L means: it should be a deflected tone but may be replaced by a level tone, L/D, vice versa.

2. If the end of first line is to contain rhyme, its tone must be level and the tone of the third character must be deflected.

b) "Level start"

L/D	L	L/D	D	D/L	r
D/L	D	D	L	L	r
D/L	D	L	L	D	
L	L	D	D	L	r
L/D	L	L	D	D	
D/L	D	D	L	L	r
D/L	D	L	L	D	
L	L	D	D	L	r

Note: In b, if the end of the first line is to contain rhyme, its tone must be level and the tone of the third character must be deflected and the tone of the first character must be level.

(B) Five-character four-line "curtailed" poem (*chüeh*):

a) "Deflected start," as the first four lines of A, a.
b) "Level start," as the first four lines of A, b.

(C) Seven-character eight-line regulated poem (*lü*):

a) "Deflected start"

D/L	D	L/D	L	L/D	D	D/L	r
L/D	L	D/L	D	D	L	L	r
L/D	L	D/L	D	L	L	D	
D/L	D	L	L	D	D	L	r
D/L	D	L/D	L	L	D	D	
L/D	L	D/L	D	D	L	L	r
L/D	L	D/L	D	L	L	D	
D/L	D	L	L	D	D	L	r

Note: In C, a, if the end of the first line is to contain rhyme, its tone must be level and the tone of the fifth character must be deflected and that of the third character must be level.

b) "Level start"

L/D	L	D/L	D	L/D	L	D/L	r
D/L	D	L	L	D	D	L	r
D/L	D	D/L	L	L	D	D	
L/D	L	D/L	D	D	L	L	r
L/D	L	D/L	D	L	L	D	
D/L	D	L	L	D	D	L	r
D/L	D	D	L	L	D	D	
L/D	L	D/L	D	D	L	L	r

Note: If the end of the first line is to contain rhyme, its tone must be level and the tone of the fifth character must be deflected.

(D) Seven-character four-line "curtailed" poem:

    a) "Deflected start," as the first four lines of C, a.
    b) "Level start," as the first four lines of C, b.

(E)

1.	LL + DD + L	(Regular)
2.	DD + LL + L	(Regular)
3.	LL + LD + D	(Regular)
4.	LL + DL + D	(Irregular)
5.	DD + LD + D	(Irregular)
6.	LL + DD + LL + D	(Regular)
7.	LL + LD + DL + L	(Regular)
8.	LL + LD + DL + L	(Regular)
9.	DL + DD + LL + D	(Regular)
10.	LL + DD + LD + D	(Irregular)
11	DD + DD + LL + D	(Irregular)

A. *WU-LÜ*

(FIVE-CHARACTER EIGHT-LINE

REGULATED POEMS)

和晉陵陸丞早春遊望

杜審言

獨有宦遊人，
偏驚物候新。
雲霞出海曙，
梅柳渡江春。
淑氣催黃鳥，
晴光轉綠蘋。
忽聞歌古調，
歸思欲霑巾。

HARMONIZING A SPRING POEM BY PREMIER LU OF CHIN-LING

Tu Shen-yen (648–708)

1. only	there-is	in-office	drifting	man
2. alone	startled	thing/s	climate	new
3. cloud/s	mist/s	go-out	sea	dawn
4. plum/s	willow/s	cross	river	spring
5. good warm	air	hurry urge-on	yellow	bird/s
6. sun	light	change	green	duckweed/s waterplant/s
7. sudden	hear	song sing	old	tune
8. return	thought	about-to	wet	lapel/s

1. Drifting officials alone
2. Would start at things new, climatic changes.
3. Clouds, mists out to sea: dawn.
4. Plums, willows across the river: spring.
5. Warm air quickens the yellow birds.
6. Sunlight turns waterplants green.
7. Suddenly, a song of ancient times
8. Swells in me tears: thoughts of home.

次北固山下　　　王灣

客路青山外
行舟綠水前
潮平兩岸闊
風正一帆懸
海日生殘夜
江春入舊年
鄉書何處達
歸雁洛陽邊

STAYOVER AT PEI-KU-SHAN *Wang Wan (693–751?)*

1. traveler	road	green	mountain	beyond
2. moving	boat	green	water	front
3. tide/s	flat calm	two	bank/s	wide(n)
4. wind	just	one	sail	straight
5. sea	sun	grow	torn, tattered receding	night
6. river	spring	enter	old (i.e., end of year)	year
7. home	letter	where	—	reach
8. returning	geese	Lo-	yang	side

1. The road reaches beyond mountains.
2. The boat moves on the green water.
3. Tides now calm: two banks widen.
4. Wind stills: one sail straight.
5. Sun grows from sea: the night tatters.
6. Upon the river, spring: the year ages.
7. A letter from home: where to send to?
8. With the returning geese to Lo-yang.

送友人　　李白

青山横北郭
白水遶東城
此地一為別
孤蓬萬里征
浮雲遊子意
落日故人情
揮手自茲去
蕭蕭班馬鳴

TAKING LEAVE OF A FRIEND　　*Li Po (701–762)*

1.	green	mountain/s	lie-across	north	outer-wall-of-city
2.	white	water	wind-around	east	city
3.	this	place	once	make	separation
4.	lone	tumbleweed	ten-thousand	mile/s	travel
5.	floating	cloud/s	wanderer	—	thought (mood)
6.	setting	sun	old	friend	feeling
7.	wave	hand/s	from	here	go
8.	*hsiao* (onomatopoeic)	*hsiao*	parting	horse	neigh

1. Green mountains lie across the north wall.
2. White water winds the east city.
3. Here once we part,
4. Lone tumbleweed; a million miles to travel.
5. Floating clouds; a wanderer's mood.
6. Setting sun; an old friend's feeling.
7. We wave hands, you go from here.
8. Neigh, neigh goes the horse at parting.

渡荆門送別　　　李白

渡遠荆門外
来從楚國遊
山隨平野盡
江入大荒流
月下飛天鏡
雲生結海樓
仍憐故鄉水
萬里送行舟

CROSSING CHING-MEN TO SEE A FRIEND OFF *Li Po*

1.	cross	distant	Ching- (place name)	men	beyond
2.	come	to; follow	Ch'u	country	roam excursion
3.	mountain/s	follow	flat	plains	end
4.	river	enter	big	wilderness	flow
5.	moon	fall/s; down	fly	sky (i.e., moon)	mirror
6.	cloud/s	grow	weave	sea (mirage)	terraces
7.	still	love	native	town	water
8.	ten-thousand	mile/s	see-off	traveling	boat

1. We cross over the distant Ching-men
2. To travel in the land of Ch'u.
3. Mountains end with vast plains.
4. River flows into the great beyond.
5. Moon falls, a mirror flying across the sky.
6. Clouds grow, weaving terraces above the sea.
7. Deep love of hometown waters:
8. A million miles to see your boat go.

聽蜀僧濬彈琴　李白

蜀僧抱綠綺
西下峨眉峰
為我一揮手
如聽萬壑松
客心洗流水
餘響入霜鐘
不覺碧山暮
秋雲暗幾重

LISTENING TO THE LUTE PLAYED BY MONK CHÜN FROM SHU *Li Po*

1.	Shu (Szechuan)	monk	hold	Green (famous lute)	Brocade
2.	west	down	Omei	—	Peak
3.	for	me	one	strum	hand
4.	like	listen	ten-thousand	valley/s	pine/s
5.	traveler	mind heart	wash(ed) rinse(d)	flowing	water
6.	remaining	sound	enter	frost	bell*
7.	not	aware of	green	mountain	dusk
8.	autumn	cloud	dark	how-many	layer/s

1. Monk Chün of Shu with a Green Brocade Lute
2. Descends from the Omei Peak.
3. A mere strumming of strings:
4. A million valleys of pines in unison.
5. A traveler's mind rinsed by flowing water.
6. A ringing continuing into a bell's echo to frost.
7. Unknowing of dusk coming over the green hills—
8. Autumn clouds darken, layers over layers. . . .
   how many?

*According to an entry in the *Classic of Mountains and Seas,* "There are nine bells in Feng Mountains which will ring when frost comes."

訪戴天山道士不遇　李白

犬吠水聲中
桃花帶雨濃
樹深時見鹿
溪午不聞鐘
野竹分青靄
飛泉挂碧峰
無人知所去
愁倚兩三松

ON VISITING TAOIST RECLUSE OF TAI-T'IEN-SHAN AND NOT FINDING HIM *Li Po*

1. dog/s	bark	water	sound	midst
2. peach	blossom/s	bring-with	rain	dense
3. tree/s	deep	at-times	see	deer
4. stream	noon	not	hear	bell
5. wild	bamboo/s	divide	green	mist
6. flying	fountain	hang	jade-green	peak
7. no	man	know	where	to
8. sad(ly)	lean-on	two	three	pine/s

1. Dogs bark in the midst of gurgling water.
2. Peach blossoms thicken with rain.
3. Deep groves: at times, a deer.
4. Stream at noon: no ringing of bell.
5. Wild bamboos share in the green mists.
6. Flying fountains hangs from the jade peak.
7. No one knows where to find him:
8. Sadly, I lean on a couple of pines.

送友人入蜀　　李白

見說蠶叢路
崎嶇不易行
山從人面起
雲傍馬頭生
芳樹籠秦棧
春流遶蜀城
升沈應已定
不必問君平

TO SEE A FRIEND OFF TO SHU* *Li Po*

1. hear	say	Ts'an-	t'sung	road
2. rugged	—	not	easy	walk
3. mountain/s	from	man's	face	rise
4. cloud/s	beside	horse	head	grow
5. fragrant	tree/s	cover overshadow	Ch'in	plank-path
6. spring	stream/s	wind (v.)	Shu	city-wall
7. ups	downs	should	already	settle(d)
8. no	need	ask	Chün	P'ing

1. They say the roads to Shu
2. Are too rugged to travel.
3. Mountains rise from the rider's face.
4. Clouds grow along the horse-head.
5. Fragrant trees shroud the plank-paths of Ch'in.
6. Freshets wind the walls of Shu.
7. Ups and downs have set courses.
8. There is no need to ask diviners.

*The roads from the capital to Shu (the present Szechuan) were tortuous and extremely difficult to travel because of sky-reaching ranges lying between them. Li Po had another poem that describes just this fact. Ts'an-ts'ung was a legendary ruler of Shu. Chün p'ing or Yen Chün-p'ing or Yen Chün was a famous diviner in Chengtu of Shu.

184

終南山　　　王維

太乙近天都
連山到海隅
白雲迴望合
青靄入看無
分野中峰變
陰晴眾壑殊
欲投人處宿
隔水問樵夫

MOUNT CHUNG-NAN　*Wang Wei (701–761)*

1.	T'ai-i (i.e., Chungnan)	near	sky	capital (i.e., imperial capital)
2.	link mountain/s	connect	sea	edge
3.	white cloud/s	turn-to-look-back		close
4.	green mist/s	enter	see	none
5.	divide wilds; land	middle	peak	change
6.	shade shine	all	valley/s	different
7.	want to-stay-over	man/'s	residence	sleep
8.	across stream; water	ask	woodcutter	—

1. Chungnan ranges near the imperial capital,
2. Mountain upon mountain to sea's brim.
3. White clouds—looking back—close up.
4. Green mists—entering—nothing.
5. Terrestrial divisions change at the middle peak.
6. Shade and light differ with every valley.
7. To stay over in some stranger's house—
8. Across the water, ask a woodcutter.

酬張少府　　王維

晚年唯好靜
萬事不關心
自顧無長策
空知返舊林
松風吹解帶
山月照彈琴
君問窮通理
漁歌入浦深

ANSWER TO VICE-PREFECT CHANG *Wang Wei*

1.	late	year/s	only	love	quietude; peace
2.	ten-thousand	affair/s matter/s	not	involve (concern)	mind
3.	self	look-into	no	long-term	plan
4.	empty	know(ledge)	return	old	woods
5.	pine	wind	blow	loosen	girdle
6.	mountain	moon	shine	strum	lute
7.	you	ask	exhaust	to-be-expert	pattern (i.e., cosmic)
8.	fisherman/'s	song	enter	estuary	deep

1. In later life, quietude my only care.
2. A million affairs, none my concern.
3. I know myself no lasting plan
4. But to go back to this old wood.
5. Pine winds blow—my girdle is loosened.
6. Mountain moon shines, I strum my lute.
7. You ask me the way to the Pattern.
8. Fisherman's song deep into the cove.

終南別業　　　王維

中　歳　頗　好　道　隨　往　知　處　時　晚
晚　家　南　山　隨　往　知　處　時
興　來　每　獨　往　知　處　時
勝　事　空　自　知　處
行　到　水　窮　林
坐　看　雲　起　還
偶　然　值　時　期
談　笑　無　還　期

VILLA AT THE FOOT OF MOUNT CHUNGNAN　*Wang Wei*

1. middle	year/s	quite	love	Buddhist-Way
2. late-years	make-home	South	Hill	side
3. impulse	come	often	alone	go
4. fine (i.e., natural scenes)	turn-of-things	in-vain	self	know
5. walk	to	water	end source	place
6. sit	see	cloud/s	rise	time
7. occasionally	—	meet	woods	old-man
8. talk	laugh	no	return	time

1. Midway in life, attuned to Buddhism.
2. Late years: a home I made at South Hill.
3. Often on impulse, I walk out by myself:
4. Magnificent scenes, I alone know;
5. Walk to the source of the stream
6. And sit down to watch clouds rise.
7. Sometimes I meet an old man in the woods
8. We talk and laugh and know no return.

山居秋暝　　王維

空山新雨後
天氣晚來秋
明月松間照
清泉石上流
竹喧歸浣女
蓮動下漁舟
隨意春芳歇
王孫自可留

AUTUMN DUSK AT A MOUNTAIN LODGE *Wang Wei*

1. empty	mountain	new	rain	after
2. sky (climate)	air	late; evening	come	autumn
3. bright	moon	pine/s	among	shine
4. clear	spring; fountain	stone/s	upon	flow
5. bamboo/s	voice/s	return	wash	girl/s
6. lotus	move	down	fisherman	boat
7. at-will	—	spring	fragrant-grass	stop
8. nobles	—	self; naturally	can	stay

1. Empty mountain after fresh rains:
2. It is evening. Autumn air rises.
3. Bright moon shines through pines.
4. Clear spring flows over stones.
5. Voices among bamboos: washing girls return.
6. Lotus-leaves move: down glide fishermen's boats.
7. Here and there, fragrant grass withers.
8. O Prince, you do not have to go.*

*Allusion to two lines in the *Ch'u Tz'u, Songs of the South,* "Summoning the Recluse": "O Prince, return! In the mountain, you should not tarry."

過香積寺

寺峰徑鍾石松曲龍
積雲人處危青潭毒
香入無何咽冷空制
過不知里木山聲色暮禪
　數古深泉日薄安

PASSING THE TEMPLE OF TEEMING FRAGRANCE *Wang Wei*

1.	not	know	Teeming-	Fragrance	Temple
2.	many	mile/s	enter	cloud/s	peak
3.	ancient	tree/s	no	man/'s	path
4.	deep	mountain	where	—	bell
5.	spring; fountain	sound	swallow; sob; choke	perilous	rock/s
6.	sun	color	cold (v.)	green	pine/s
7.	dusk	—	empty	pool	bend
8.	pacify (i.e., practice Ch'an or Zen)	Ch'an	exorcise	poisonous	dragon

1. Where is the Temple of Teeming Fragrance?
2. Miles and miles into cloud-peaks.
3. Ancient trees: no man's path.
4. Deep in the mountains: where, this bell?
5. Fountain sob, swallowing perilous rocks.
6. Sun's color chills green pines.
7. Dusk. At an empty pool's bend,
8. Meditation exorcises heart's virulent dragon.

漢江臨汎　　王維

楚塞三湘接
荊門九派通
江流天地外
山色有無中
郡邑浮前浦
波瀾動遠空
襄陽好風日
留醉與山翁

FLOATING ON THE RIVER HAN *Wang Wei*

1.	Ch'u	Ford Pass	three	Hsiang-waters	connect
2.	Ching- (or Bramble Gate)	men	nine	tributaries	go-through
3.	river	flow	sky	earth	beyond
4.	mountain	color	being	not-being	middle
5.	cities	town	float	front	bank
6.	wave/s	billow/s	move	distant	sky
7.	Hsiang	Yang	good	wind	sun
8.	leave-behind	drunk	with	Shan (i.e., Shan Chien of the Chin Dynasty)	old-man

1. Ford of Ch'u, knot for three Hsiang waters.
2. Bramble Gate, through which nine tributaries go.
3. The river flows beyond the sky and earth.
4. The mountain's color, between seen and unseen.
5. Cities float before the bank.
6. Waves move the distant sky.
7. In Hsiang-yang, a gorgeous day today.
8. Get drunk with Shan Chien of Chin.*

*Shan Chien was a famous drunkard, often in the midst of an excursion.

春望　　　杜甫

國破山河在
城春草木深
感時花濺淚
恨別鳥驚心
烽火連三月
家書抵萬金
白頭搔更短
渾欲不勝簪

SPRING SCENE *Tu Fu (712–770)*

1.	empire	broken	mountain/s	river	exist; remain
2.	city	spring	grass	tree/s	thick; deep
3.	feel	times	flower/s	splash	tear/s
4.	hate; distressed by	separation	bird/s	startle	heart
5.	beacon	fire/s	continue	three	month/s
6.	home	letter	equal/s	ten-thousand	taels
7.	white	head	scratch	even	short/er
8.	simply	—	not	able-to-hold	pin

1. All ruins, the empire; mountains and rivers in view.
2. To the city, spring: grass and trees so thick.
3. The times strike. Before flowers, tears break loose.
4. Separation cuts. Birds startle our heart.
5. Beacon fires continued for three months on end.
6. A letter from home is worth thousands of gold pieces.
7. White hair, scratched, becomes thinner and thinner,
8. So thin it can hardly hold a pin.

春宿左省　　　杜甫

花隱掖垣暮
啾啾棲鳥過
星臨萬戶動
月傍九霄多
不寢聽金鑰
因風想玉珂
明朝有封事
數問夜如何

SPRING VIGIL IN THE IMPERIAL CHANCELLERY *Tu Fu*

1. flower/s	lurk	palace-wall/s	wall/s	dusk
2. *chiu* (onomatopoeic)	*chiu*	resting nest-coming	bird/s	pass-by
3. star/s	come	ten-thousand	household/s	move
4. moon	beside	nine-	sky	more
5. not	asleep	hear	gold key/s (i.e., bronze-tracery)	key/s
6. because-of	wind	think	jade	pendant
7. tomorrow	morning	have	sealed	business
8. many-times	ask	night	how	—

1. Flowers lurk in the dusk by the palace walls.
2. Twitter, twitter, homing birds pass by.
3. Stars come: a million houses move.
4. The moon by the empyrean seems to be much more.
5. Sleepless: golden keys ring.
6. On the wind, jade pendants seem to tinkle.
7. Tomorrow morning I have a sealed petition to make.
8. All night long I ask: what has become of the night?

初月　　　　　杜甫

光細弦欲上
影斜輪未安
微升古塞外
已隱暮雲端
河漢不改色
關山空自寒
庭前有白露
暗滿菊花團

NEW MOON *Tu Fu*

1. ray/s	slender	quarter	about-to	first
		(i.e., about to be in its first quarter)		
2. shadow	aslant	ring	not-yet	stable
3. barely	rise	ancient	fortress	beyond
		(i.e., beyond the ancient fortress)		
4. already	lurk	evening	cloud/s	edge
5. milky	way	not	change	color
6. pass	mountain	empty	by-itself	cold
(mountain pass)*				
7. courtyard	front	there-is	white	dew
8. dark; secretly	fill; full	chrysanthemum/s	—	heavy-with-dew (drenched)

1. Slender rays: a chord barely seen.
2. Slanting shadows; its rings not yet stable.
3. Rising from beyond the Ancient Fortress,
4. It lurks behind evening clouds' edge.
5. The Milky Way does not change its color.
6. The mountain pass is cold, void, all by itself.
7. There is white dew before the courtyard
8. Dabbling the chrysanthemums in the dark.

*Traditionally, "mountains within the country."

月夜　　　杜甫

今閨遙未香清何雙
夜中憐解霧輝時照
鄜只小憶雲玉依淚
州獨兒長鬟臂虛痕
月看女安濕寒幌乾

MOONLIT NIGHT *Tu Fu*

1.	this	night	Fu	Chou's	moon
2.	boudoir	middle	only	alone	watch
3.	at-a-distance	pity	small	son	daughter
4.	not-yet	know	remember	Ch'ang	An
5.	fragrant	mist	cloud	hair	wet
6.	clear	ray	jade (i.e., white)	arm	cold
7.	what	time	lean-on	empty false	curtain
8.	double	shine	tear	mark	dry

1. Tonight, moon over Fu-chou.
2. My wife watches it alone there.
3. I think of my children across such distance;
4. They don't understand why I am in Ch'ang-an.
5. Fragrant mist wets cloud-locks.
6. Clear moonlight chills white arms.
7. When can we lean on the open casement together,
8. Doubly shone, as tears dry up?

夜宴左氏莊　　　杜甫

風林纖月落
衣露淨琴張
暗水流花徑
春星帶草堂
檢書燒燭短
看劍引盃長
詩罷聞吳詠
扁舟意不忘

NIGHT FEAST AT THE TSOS *Tu Fu*

1.	wind	forest	slender	moon	fall
2.	cloth	dew dew-dabbled dew-dappled	pure; clean	lute	lay-out
3.	dark	water	flow	flower	path
4.	spring	star/s	belt (v.)	thatch	house
5.	examine peruse	book	burn	candle	short
6.	examine	sword	hold	cup	long-time
7.	poem	finished	hear	Wu	tune
8.	small	boat	idea	not	forget

1. Windblown forest: the slender moon has fallen.
2. Cloth dew-dabbled, the lute stands there untouched.
3. Dark water flows among flower-paths.
4. Spring stars belt the thatched house.
5. We leaf over books, to find candles short-burnt.
6. We show off swords: drink cups and cups of wine.
7. Poems done: hear the accent of Wu:
8. Go a-boating is the idea never to forget.*

*Fan-li, after having succeeded in helping the King of Yüeh to overthrow the King of Wu, retreated from public life and went a-boating.

春日憶李白　　　　　杜甫

白也詩無敵，飄然思不群。
清新庾開府，俊逸鮑參軍。
渭北春天樹，江東日暮雲。
何時一樽酒，重與細論文。

SPRING DAY: THINKING OF LI PO *Tu Fu*

1.	Po	(part.)	poetry	no	match
2.	soaring untrammeled	—	thought	not	common
3.	clear	fresh	Yü	K'ai (i.e., the official title Yü Hsin holds, referring honorifically to the man himself)	Fu
4.	vigorous outstanding	flowing	Pao (i.e., Pao Chao)	T'san	Chün
5.	Wei	north	spring (i.e., spring season)	day	tree/s
6.	river	east	day	dusk	cloud/s
7.	what	time	one	vessel jar; bottle	wine
8.	again	with to-great-detail	closely	discuss	literature belles lettres

1. Li Po's poetry: no match anywhere.
2. Soaring, his imagination always above others.
3. Clear, fresh like Yü Hsin.
4. Vigorous, free-flowing like Pao Chao.
5. North of River Wei: trees of spring.
6. East of the Yangtze: clouds of sundown.
7. When can we talk about literature again
8. Over a bottle of wine?

杜甫

山開塞闌岷遷望顏
重谷出臨何末長摧
萬山雲月歸斬一正
州芥城風夜國蘭塵颯
秦芥孤無不屬樓烟哀

詩

州

雜

秦

FROM MISCELLANEOUS POEMS OF CH'IN-CHOU *Tu Fu*

1.	vast (disorder)	— —	ten-thousand	layer/s	mountain/s
2.	lone	city castle	mountain	valley	middle
3.	no	wind	cloud	emerge	fortress
4.	not	night	moon	hover-over arrive-at	pass
5.	Vassal State (i.e., Su-wu, the well-known Han envoy's official title)		return	how	late
6.	Lou Lan (i.e., Fu Chieh-tzu, who has the king of Lou Lan beheaded for allying with the Huns)	Lan	beheading	not-yet	return
7.	smoke (i.e., bonfire)	dust	alone	long-time	watch
8.	spent decaying	wind	now	destroy ravage	face

1. A chaos of mountains upon mountains.
2. Among them, in a valley, an isolated city.
3. No wind: clouds driven out of the fortress.
4. Not even night: the moon looms over the pass.
5. Why is the envoy so late in his return?
6. To await the killing of the barbarian chief?
7. Smoke-dust across such vast space:
8. Spent wind is ravaging my face.

B. *CH'I-LÜ*

(SEVEN-CHARACTER EIGHT-LINE

REGULATED POEMS)

登金陵鳳皇臺　李白

鳳皇臺上鳳皇遊
鳳去臺空江自流
吳宮花草埋幽徑
晉代衣冠成古丘
三山半落青天外
二水中分白鷺洲
總為浮雲能蔽日
長安不見使人愁

1. phoenix	—	terrace	upon	phoenix	—	play; excursion
(on the phoenix terrace)						
2. phoenix	gone	terrace	empty	river	alone	flow
3. Wu	palace	flower/s	grass; weeds	bury	dark secluded	path
4. Chin	Dynasty	gown/s	cap/s*	become	old	mound
5. three	mountain/s	half	fall	blue	sky	beyond
6. two	water/s; river/s	middle	divide	white	egret	isle
7. always	because	floating	clouds	can	cover	sun
8. Ch'angan	—	not	see	make	man	sad

1. On the phoenix terrace, phoenix at play.
2. Phoenix gone; terrace empty; the river flows on alone.
3. Wu Palace: flowers and weeds bury the dark paths.
4. Robes and caps of Chin Dynasty have gone into grave mounds.
5. The Three Mountains half-falling beyond the sky,
6. White Egret Isle splits the river into two.
7. Always, floating clouds cover the sun:
8. No sight of Ch'angan: sorrow, sorrow.

*Synecdoche for officials of high-ranking positions

閣夜　　　　杜甫

歲暮陰陽催短景
天涯霜雪霽寒宵
五更鼓角聲悲壯
三峽星河影動搖
野哭幾家聞戰伐
夷歌數處起漁樵
臥龍躍馬終黃土
人事音書漫寂寥

NIGHT UP IN THE TOWER *Tu Fu*

1. year	dusk	yin	yang*	hurry	short	(day)light
2. sky's	edge	frost	snow	clear (v.)	cold	night
3. fifth	watch	drum/s	horn/s	sound	sad	brave
4. three	gorge/s	star	river (Milky Way)	shadow	move	shake
5. wilds	weeping	thousand	home/s	hear	warfare	—
6. barbar-ian	song/s	several	place/s	rise	fishermen	wood-cutters
7. lying; sleeping	dragon	leaping	horse†	end-with	yellow	dust
8. human	affair/s	message/s	letter/s	let-it-be	silent	solitary

1. Dusking year, in cosmic measure, ushers in shorter days.
2. Beyond the horizon, snow clears up: a freezing night.
3. Fifth watch: drums and bugles of splitting grief.
4. At the Three Gorges: river of stars, trembling shadows.
5. In the wilds, weeping: a million homes with thudding of war.
6. Barbarian songs, here and there, rise with fishermen, woodcutters
7. Sleeping Dragon, Leaping Horse, now with yellow dust—
8. Human affairs, family letters: O let silence. . . .

*Yin-yang, the two cosmic forces, one complementing the other, that give rise to all phenomena (and changes) in the universe.

†Sleeping Dragon is Chu-ko Liang (181–234), famous statesman in the Three Kingdoms Period, so named because he lived in Sleeping Dragon Hill before he joined Liu Pei in an effort to restore the Han Dynasty. Leaping Horse, nickname of Kung-sun Shu, ruler of the Szechuan area in the first century.

客至　　　　杜甫

舍南見逕門쒌酒與籤

舍但花蓬盤樽肯隔

舍群不今市鄰呼

北鷗曾始遠貧翁取

皆日緣滿無只相盡

春日客君秉舊對餘

水来掃開味醅飲杯

A GUEST   *Tu Fu*

1.	house	south	house	north	all	spring	water
2.	but	see	flock	gull/s	day (every day)	day	come
3.	flower	path	not	once	due-to	guest	sweep
4.	thatch	door	now	then	for	you	open
5.	dish	food	market	far	no	include (variety of food)	taste/s
6.	bottle	wine	home	poor	only	old	home-brew
7.	willing	with	neighbor	old-man	mutual- (drink to each other)	face	drink
8.	across	fence	call	get	finish	remaining	cup

1. South of house, north of house, all spring water.
2. Day in, day out, flights of gulls come.
3. Petal-strewn path never once swept to welcome guests.
4. The thatched gate, for the first time, is opened for you.
5. Far from market, dishes have to be few.
6. Now poor, for wine, nothing but old home-brew.
7. Willing to toast to the old man next door?
8. Across the fence, let's call him to help finish the cups.

聞官軍收河南河北　杜甫

劍外忽傳收薊北，初聞涕淚滿衣裳。
卻看妻子愁何在，漫卷詩書喜欲狂。
白日放歌須縱酒，青春作伴好還鄉。
即從巴峽穿巫峽，便下襄陽向洛陽。

HEARING OF IMPERIAL FORCES RETAKING HO-NAN AND HO-PEI *Tu Fu*

1.	Chien (in Szechuan)	beyond	sudden	hear	retake	Chi (in Ho-pei)	north
2.	first	hear	tear/s	tear/s	all-over	clothes	—
3.	turn-head	see	wife	—	sad	where	is
4.	unaware	roll	poem	book	glee	about-to	mad
5.	white	day	release	song	must	indulge	wine
6.	green	spring	to-be	companion	good	return	home
7.	imme-diately	from	Pa	Gorge	through	Wu	Gorge
8.	then	down	Hsiang-	yang	toward	Lo-	yang

1. At Chien-nan, sudden news of retaking Chi-pei.
2. Overjoyed tears all over my clothes.
3. I peep at my wife: where is her sadness?
4. Rolling up scrolls of books: glee edges into madness.
5. A robust song in broad daylight: wine unlimited.
6. Spring be our companion, all merry to go home.
7. At once from Pa Gorge through Wu Gorge
8. Down Hsiang-yang toward Lo-yang.

登高　　　　　杜甫

風急天高猿嘯哀　渚清沙白鳥飛迴
無邊落木蕭蕭下　不盡長江滾滾來
萬里悲秋常作客　百年多病獨登臺
艱難苦恨繁霜鬢　潦倒新停濁酒杯

CLIMBING ON THE DOUBLE NINTH DAY *Tu Fu*

1.	wind/s	severe	sky	high	gibbon/s	cry	sad
2.	shore; water	clear	sand	white	bird/s	fly	circle
3.	no	edge	leaf-falling	tree/s	*hsiao*	*hsiao* (onomatopoeic)	down
4.	no	end	long (Yangtze)	river	rolling	rolling	come
5.	ten-thousand	mile/s	sad grieve	autumn	always	be	traveler
6.	hundred	year/s	much	sickness	alone	ascend	terrace
7.	hard-ship/s	—	bitter	regrets	complex propagate	frost	side-temple-hair
8.	wretched-state		fresh; recent	stop	turbulent	wine	cup

1. Shrill winds, high sky, monkeys' heart-rending cry.
2. Clear river, white sand, birds soar and wheel.
3. Leaves, leaves of a rimless forest rustle down.
4. Waves upon waves, the endless Yangtze comes drumming in.
5. A million miles of grievous autumn, constantly a traveler.
6. Entire life in sickness: I alone climb up the terrace.
7. Hardships, bitter regrets propagates my frosty hair.
8. Wretched! that I have recently stopped going for the cup!

錦瑟　　李商隱

錦瑟無端五十絃
一絃一柱思華年
莊生曉夢迷蝴蝶
望帝春心託杜鵑
滄海月明珠有淚
藍田日暖玉生煙
此情可待成追憶
祇是當時已惘然

THE INLAID LUTE *Li Shang-yin (812?–58)*

1.	Chin- (i.e., inlaid lute)	se	no	reason	fif-	ty	string/s
2.	one	string	one	peg	think; recall	flower(y)	year/s
3.	Chuang (i.e., Chuangtzu)*	Sheng	morning	dream	fascinated-by	butterfly	—
4.	Wang-	ti†	spring	heart	change/s; transform/s	nightjar	—
5.	vast	sea	moon	bright	pearl/s	has	tear/s
6.	blue	field	sun	warm	jade	grow(s)	smoke
7.	this	feeling	can (does it need . . .)	wait	to-become	pursue	memory
8.	but		at-the-moment	already		lost	(as in fog)

1. How come the inlaid lute has fifty strings?
2. One string, one peg: surges of flowery years.
3. Chuangtzu wakes up, charmed by dream of a butterfly.
4. Wangti, in spring, returns as a nightjar.
5. Dark sea: bright moon: pearls with tears.
6. Blue fields: warm sun: jade engenders smoke.
7. This feeling: does it have to wait to be memory?
8. This moment as it comes: already lost as in trance.

*Once Chuang Chou (i.e., Chuangtzu who is also the speaker of this passage) dreamt that he was a butterfly. . . . Is it Chuang who dreamt that he was a butterfly or the butterfly who dreamt that it was Chuang?

†Wangti sent Pieh Ling to deal with the floods, and debauched his wife. He was ashamed, and considering Pieh Ling a better man than himself, abdicated the state to him. At the time when Wangti left, the nightjar began to call. That is why the nightjar's call is sad to the people of Shu and reminds them of Wangti. . . . When Wangti died his soul turned into a bird called the "nightjar."—summarized from Yang Hsiung and others by A. C. Graham

無 題　　李商隱

昨夜星辰昨夜風　東翼通暖紅去蓬

夜堂雙飛點酒燈官斷

昨桂雙一春蠟應類

辰畔鳳犀鉤覆鼓臺

星西彩靈送射聽蘭

夜樓無有座賮余馬

昨畫身心隔分嗟走

214

WITHOUT TITLE (I) *Li Shang-yin*

1.	last	night	star/s	—	last	night	wind/s
2.	painted	chamber	west	side	cassia	hall	east
3.	body	no	colorful	phoenix('s)	pair	fly	wing/s
4.	heart	there-is	magic	horn	one	point	communicated
5.	separate	table	send (game)	hook	spring	wine	warm
6.	divide	team/s	guess (game,riddle)	"covered"	candle	lamp	red
7.	alas	I	hear	drum	respond	official	go
8.	run	horse	orchid	terrace	like	uprooted	tumble-weed

1. Last night's stars, last night's winds.
2. West of the painted chamber, east of the cassia hall.
3. My body: no wings of a gorgeous soaring phoenix.
4. Our hearts: a point illuminated through the magic horn.*
5. Across the table, play "hook-a-turtle": spring wine is warmed.
6. In teams, try "tongue-twisters": candles burn red.
7. Too bad! The drum calls me to my duties.
8. I rush my horse to the Orchid Terrace:† an uprooted tumbleweed.

*The rhinoceros was believed to be divine and magical because of its horns, which were supposed to contain in them a white line running from one end to the other, a figure to mean "no blockade between."
†Imperial Secretariat.

無題　　　　　李商隱

相見時難別亦難，
東風無力百花殘。
春蠶到死絲方盡，
蠟炬成灰淚始乾。
曉鏡但愁雲鬢改，
夜吟應覺月光寒。
蓬萊此去無多路，
青鳥殷勤為探看。

WITHOUT TITLE (II) *Li Shang-yin*

1. meeting	—	time	hard	separation	also	hard
2. east	wind	no	strength	hundred	flower/s	wither
3. spring	silkworm	till	death	silk	then	end (v.)
4. candle/s	—	become	ash	tear/s	then	dry
5. morning	mirror/s	but	sad	cloud-	hair	change
6. night	chant (poems)	should	feel	moon	light	chill
7. Penglai (fairyland)	—	this	go	not	much	road (-to-go)
8. blue	bird	attentive	—	for	find-out	(news/ way)

1. Meeting is hard. Harder, separation.
2. East wind now powerless, all flowers wither.
3. Spring silkworms' thread ends with their death.
4. Candles will not dry their tears until they turn ashes.
5. Before morning mirrors: sad that cloud-hair may fade.
6. Chanting poems at night: feel the moonlight's chill?
7. Penglai's fairyland is not too far.*
8. Blue Bird, be attentive, sound out the way.†

*Penglai, isles of the blessed, where three Sacred Mountains were located.
†Blue Bird, a messenger of the goddess Queen Mother of the West.

春雨　　　　　李商隱

悵臥新春白袷衣，白門寥落意多違。
紅樓隔雨相望冷，珠箔飄燈獨自歸。
遠路應悲春晼晚，殘宵猶得夢依稀。
玉璫緘札何由達，萬里雲羅一雁飛。

SPRING RAIN *Li Shang-yin*

1.	mope	in-bed	new	spring	white	short-	coat
2.	white	door	deserted forlorn	—	wish(es)	much	at-odds
3.	red	chamber	blocked -by	rain	mutual	watch	cold
4.	beaded	blind	floating rocking	lamp	alone	by-oneself	return
5.	distant	road	must	bemoan	spring	sunset	late
6.	remaining	night	still	get	dream	seem-&-seem-not	
7.	jade	earring/s	letter	—	where	to	reach
8.	ten-thousand	mile	cloud-	net	one	goose	fly

1. I mope the new spring away in a white coat.
2. White Gate dilapidated: odds are always against us.
3. Across the rains, the red chamber looks cold.
4. Beaded blind, rocking lamp, I return all alone.
5. Road so remote, should you not grieve the dusking spring?
6. Last hours of the night: still a dream, seeming, not to seem.
7. Jade earrings, letters, where and how to send?
8. Across a million miles of cloud-net, a single goose flies.

宿晉昌亭聞驚禽　李商隱

羈緒鰥鰥夜景侵，高窗不掩見驚禽。
飛來曲渚煙方合，過盡南塘樹更深。
胡馬嘶和榆塞笛，楚猿吟雜橘村砧。
失群掛木知何限，遠隔天涯共此心。

HEARING A STARTLED BIRD DURING STAYOVER AT CHIN-CH'ANG PAVILION *Li Shang-yin*

1.	travel-worn	confused-thread	fish-eyes (manner of sleepless, wide open eyes)		night	scene	attack enter
2.	high	window	not	shut	see	startled	bird
3.	fly-	here	meandering	shore	smoke	just	close
4.	pass	all	South	Pond	tree/s	more	deep
5.	Tartar	horse/s	neigh	go-with	Elm	Pass	flute/s
6.	Ch'u (Southland)	monkey/s	cry	mix	Orange	Village	pound-and-wash*
7.	lost (ref. bird)	company	hang	tree	know	what	limit end
8.	distant	blocked-by	sky	edge	share	this	heart

1. Wayworn: wide sleepless eyes. A night scene enters.
2. A high open window reveals a startled bird.
3. It flies to the meandering shore: smoke closes in.
4. It passes the South Pond: trees darken their depth.
5. Tartar horses neigh to the flutes of the Elm Pass.
6. Southland monkeys' howl mixes with the pound-and-wash.
7. Stray bird up on the tree: does it know its end?
8. Separated by sky's edge: we share this moment this heart.

*Traditional motif, refers to the washing of clothes (to be sent to the frontier guards) by women by the river, often involving the use of a club.

C. *WU-CHÜEH*

(FIVE-CHARACTER FOUR-LINE

"CURTAILED" POEMS)

鳥 鳴 磵　　　王 維

落 花 桂 閑 人
空 山 春 靜 夜
鳥 山 驚 出 月
中 澗 春 鳴 時

BIRD-SINGING STREAM   *Wang Wei*

1.	man	leisure	cassia	flower	fall
2.	quiet	night	spring	mountain	empty
3.	moon	rise	startle	mountain	bird
4.	at-times	sing	spring	stream	middle

1. Man at leisure. Cassia flowers fall.
2. Quiet night. Spring mountain is empty.
3. Moon rises. Startles—a mountain bird.
4. It sings at times in the spring stream.

鹿柴　　　王維

空山不見人
但聞人語響
返景入深林
復照青苔上

FOUR EXAMPLES FROM THE POEMS OF RIVER WANG
DEER ENCLOSURE *Wang Wei*

1. empty	mountain	not	see	man
2. but	hear	man/'s	voice	sound
3. reflecting	shadow	enter	deep	forest
(i.e., sun's reflection)				
4. again	shine	green	moss	upon
and				

1. Empty mountain: no man.
2. But voices of men are heard.
3. Sun's reflections reaches into the woods
4. And shines upon the green moss.

竹 里 館　　　　王 維

獨 坐 幽 篁 裡
彈 琴 復 長 嘯
深 林 人 不 相 知
明 月 來 相 照

BAMBOO GROVE *Wang Wei*

1.	alone	sit	dark secluded	bamboo/s	among
2.	strum	lute	and again	long	whistle
3.	deep	forest	man	not	know
4.	bright	moon	come	mutual-each-other	shine*

1. I sit alone among dark bamboos,
2. Strum the lute and let loose my voice.
3. Grove so deep, no one knows.
4. The moon visits and shines on me.

*(1) to keep him company by shining; (2) illumination; (3) the primary meaning of shining.

樂家瀬　　　　王維

颯颯秋雨中
淺淺石溜瀉
跳波自相濺
白鷺驚復下

RILL OF THE HOUSE OF THE LUANS *Wang Wei*

1. blast-blast	—	autumn	rain/s	middle
2. lightly-lightly shallow-shallow	—	rock	flow	pour
3. jump	wave/s bead/s	self	mutual each other	splash
4. white	egret	startle	again	down

1. Blasts of wind amidst autumn rains,
2. *Patter-patter* upon rocky clod.
3. Jumping beads splash against each other.
4. A white egret—startled—then down.

辛夷塢　　王維

木末芙蓉花
山中發紅萼
澗戶寂無人
紛紛開且落

HSIN-I VILLAGE *Wang Wei*

1.	tree	tip	hibiscus	—	flower
2.	mountain	middle	set-forth	red	calyx
3.	stream	hut; home	still; silent	no	man
4.	profuse-	profuse	open	and	fall

1. High on tree-tips, the hibiscus.
2. In the mountain sets forth red calyxes.
3. A home by a stream, quiet. No man.
4. It blooms and falls, blooms and falls.

山中

荊溪白石出
天寒紅葉稀
山路元無雨
空翠溼人衣

IN THE MOUNTAIN   *Wang Wei*

1.	Ching Bramble	Stream	white	stone/s pebble/s	jut-out
2.	sky weather	cold	red	leaves	sparse
3.	mountain	path road	originally	no	rain
4.	sky; empty sky-high	jade-green greenery	wet	man/'s	clothes

1. In the Bramble Stream, white stones stick out.
2. Cold weather: red leaves are sparse.
3. No rain along the mountain path.
4. Skyward greenery wets one's clothes.

春　曉　　　　孟浩然

春眠不覺曉
處處聞啼鳥
夜來風雨聲
花落知多少

SPRINGTIME SLEEP   *Meng Hao-jan (699–740)*

1.	spring	sleep	not	aware-of	dawn
2.	everywhere	—	hear	singing	bird/s
3.	night (since last night)	come	wind	rain	sound
4.	flower/s	fall	know	how	many

1. Springtime sleep: too deep to know dawn.
2. Everywhere, birds sing.
3. Entire last night: winds and rains.
4. Falling flowers: how many?

宿建德江　　孟浩然

移舟泊烟渚
日暮客愁新
野曠天低樹
江清月近人

STAYOVER AT CHIEN-TEH RIVER *Meng Hao-jan*

1.	move	boat	moor	smoke	shore
2.	sun	dusk	traveler	grief	new
3.	wilds (vast wilderness)	far-reaching	sky	low/er	tree
4.	river	clear	moon	near/s	man

1. A boat slows, moors by beach-run in smoke.
2. Sun fades: a traveler's sorrow freshens.
3. Open wilderness. Wide sky. A stretch of low trees.
4. Limpid river: clear moon close to man.

Another:
A boat slows,
moors by
beach-run in smoke.
Sun fades:
a traveler's sorrow
freshens.
Open wilderness.
Wide sky.
A stretch of low trees.
Limpid river:
clear moon
close to
man.

絕句二首　　　　杜甫

遲　日　江　山　麗
春　風　花　草　香
泥　融　飛　鶯　子
沙　暖　睡　鴛　鴦

WU-CHÜEH: TWO POEMS *Tu Fu*

NO. 1

1. late	sun	river/s	mountain/s	beautiful
2. spring	wind/s	flower/s	grass	fragrant
3. soil	thaw	fly	swallow/s	—
4. sand	warm	sleep	drake-and-	duck

1. Lingering sun: rivers and mountains brighten.
2. Spring winds: flowers and grass give out scent.
3. Soil thaws and swallows fly.
4. On the warm sand sleeping, drake-and-duck.

江碧鳥逾白
山青花欲燃
今春看又過
何日是歸年

NO. 2

1.	river	jade-green	bird/s	more	white
2.	mountain/s	green	flower/s	about-to	burn
3.	this	spring	see	again	pass (-away)
4.	which (when)	day	is	return	year

1. Jade river: birds are dazzling white and whiter.
2. Green mountains: flowers seem to flame.
3. This spring: look! is going.
4. What day is the day of return?

江　雪　　　　柳宗元

千　山　鳥　飛　絶
萬　徑　人　踪　滅
孤　舟　簑　笠　翁
獨　釣　寒　江　雪

RIVER SNOW　*Liu Tsung-yuan (773–819)*

1.	thousand	mountain/s	bird	fly; flight	cut-off
2.	ten-thousand	path/s	man	trace	extinct
3.	lone	boat	bamboo-leaved-raincoat	bamboo-leaved-hat	old man
4.	alone	fish (v.)	cold	river	snow

1. A thousand mountains—no bird's flight.
2. A million paths—no man's trace.
3. Single boat. Bamboo-leaved cape. An old man
4. Fishing by himself: ice-river. Snow.

登 鸛 雀 樓　　王之渙

白 日 依 山 盡
黃 河 入 海 流
欲 窮 千 里 目
更 上 一 層 樓

ASCEND THE HERON TOWER　*Wang Chih-huan (695–?)*

1.	white	sun	follow	mountain	end
2.	yellow	river	enter	sea	flow
3.	to; want	exhaust	thousand	mile	eye sight
4.	again once more	up	one (one more flight of stairs)	level	tower

1. White sun ends with the mountains.
2. Yellow River flows on into the sea.
3. To widen the ken of a thousand miles,
4. Up, up another flight of stairs.

秋夜寄丘二十二員外　韋應物

懷君屬秋夜
散步詠涼天
山空松子落
幽人應未眠

AUTUMN NIGHT: A LETTER SENT TO CH'IU

Wei Ying-wu (773–828)

1.	think-of	you	belong	autumn	night
2.	stroll	—	chant	cool	sky
3.	empty	mountain	pine	cone/s	fall
4.	secluded	man	must	not-yet	sleep

1. Thinking of you, in autumn night,
2. Strolling, chanting the cool air.
3. Empty mountain: pine cones fall.
4. Secluded man: staying up, still?

D. *CH'I-CHÜEH*

(SEVEN-CHARACTER FOUR-LINE

"CURTAILED" POEMS)

黄鶴樓送孟浩然之廣陵

故人　西辭黄鶴樓　李白
煙花　三月下揚州
孤帆遠影碧空盡
唯見長江天際流

TO SEE MENG HAO-JAN OFF TO YANG-CHOU *Li Po*

1.	old	friend	west	depart*	Yellow	Crane	Tower
2.	smoke	flower	third	month	down	Yang	Chou
3.	lone	sail	distant	shade	blue	sky	end (v.)
4.	only	see	long	river	sky	end	flow
			(the Yangtze)				

1. My old friend takes off from the Yellow Crane Tower,
2. In smoke-flower third month down to Yangchou.
3. A lone sail, a distant shade, lost in the blue horizon.
4. Only the long Yangtze is seen flowing into the sky.

*i.e., goes east.

春夜洛城聞笛　　李白
誰家玉笛暗飛聲
散入春風滿洛城
此夜曲中聞折柳
何人不起故園情

**HEARING THE FLUTE IN THE CITY OF LOYANG
IN A SPRING NIGHT** *Li Po*

1. whose	house	jade	flute	dark invisible subdued	flying fleeting	sound
2. scatter	enter	spring	wind/s	fill	Lo	City
3. this	night	tune	middle	hear	break (name of a tune)	willow*
4. what	man	not	arouse move stir	old- (home)	garden	thought feeling

1. Whose jade-flute is this, notes flying invisibly
2. Scatter into spring winds, filling City of Loyang?
3. Hearing the "Break-a-Willow-Twig" tonight,
4. Who can withhold the surge of thoughts of home?

*Break a willow twig for a parting gift.

閨　怨　　　王昌齡

閨中少婦不知愁
春日凝妝上翠樓
忽見陌頭楊柳色
悔教夫婿覓封侯

COMPLAINT FROM A LADY'S CHAMBER
Wang Ch'ang-ling (698–765?)

1. lady's-chamber	midst	young	lady	not	know	sadness
2. spring	day	full	makeup	ascend	jade green	tower
3. suddenly	see	field	head	willow	—	color
4. regret	to-have-advised	husband	—	seek	high-titles-such-as lord, duke, etc.	

1. In the chamber the lady knows no sadness.
2. Spring day, dressed up, she climbs a tower of jade.
3. She sees suddenly the willow's green in the fields
4. And regrets having sent her husband to seek imperial titles.

240

楓 橋 夜 泊　　　張 繼

月 落 烏 啼 霜 滿 天
江 楓 漁 火 對 愁 眠
姑 蘇 城 外 寒 山 寺
夜 半 鐘 聲 到 客 船

NIGHT-MOORING AT MAPLE BRIDGE

Chang Chi (?–780)

1. moon	down	crow/s	caw	frost	full	sky
2. river	maple	fishing	lamp/s	facing	sad	sleep
3. Ku	Su	City	beyond	Cold	Mountain	Temple

(i.e., beyond Ku-su; Su-chou City)

4. mid-	night	bell	ringing	to	visitor	boat

1. Moondown: crows caw. Frost, a skyful.
2. River maples, fishing lamps, sad drowsiness.
3. Beyond Su-chou City, the Cold Mountain Temple
4. Rings its midnight bell, reaching this visitor's boat.

泊秦淮　　　杜　牧

烟籠寒水月籠沙
夜泊秦淮近酒家
商女不知亡國恨
隔江猶唱後庭花

MOORING AT RIVER CH'IN-HUAI　*Tu Mu (803–952)*

1.	smoke	shroud	cold	water	moon	shroud	sand
2.	night	moor	Ch'in	Huai	near	wine	shop
			(River Ch'in-huai)				
3.	merchant	daughter/s	not	know	lost	kingdom	grief
4.	across	river	still	sing	Rear	Court	Flower/s

1. Smoke shrouds cold water, moonlight shrouds sand.
2. Night-mooring at Ch'in-huai, close to wineshops.
3. Gay girls know no lost kingdom's sadness.
4. Still sing across the river "Jade Flowers in Rear Court."*

*Emperor Chen Hou-chu (the last emperor of Chen, 583–587) indulged in sensual music and asked his courtiers to compose many sensual lyrics. Among them the most famous was "Jade Flowers in Rear Court."

夜雨寄北　　李商隱

君問歸期未有期
巴山夜雨漲秋池
何當共剪西窗燭
卻話巴山夜雨時

NIGHT RAINS: A LETTER TO GO NORTH

Li Shang-yin

1. you	ask	return	date	not-yet	have	date
2. Pa	Shan Mountain	night	rain	swell	autumn	pool
3. (when	can)	together	trim	west	window	candle
4. but	talk	Pa	Shan	night	rain	time

1. You ask: when to return? Don't know when.
2. Pa Shan's night rains swell autumn pools.
3. When can we trim candles together at West Window
4. And talk of Pa Shan, Pa Shan of night rains?

嫦 娥　　　李商隱

雲母屏風燭影深
長河漸落曉星沉
嫦娥應悔偷靈藥
碧海青天夜夜心

CH'ANG-O *Li Shang-yin*

1.	cloud-(mica)	mother	standing-	screen/s	candle	shadow/s	deep
2.	long (i.e., Milky Way)	river	gradually	fall	morning	star/s	sink
3.	Ch'ang	O	should	regret	steal	magic	potion
4.	green	sea	blue	sky	night	night	heart

1. Upon mica screens, candles flicker deep shadows.
2. The long Milky Way fades. Morning stars sink.
3. Ch'ang-O must be sorry for stealing the magic potion—*
4. Green sea, blue sky, thinking night after night in throes.

*Ch'ang-O, ill-treated by her husband Hou I, stole the herb of immortality and fled to the moon where she got stranded and became the goddess of the moon.

KU-SHIH: **POEMS AFTER**

THE STYLE OF ANCIENT POEMS

INCLUDING THE LITERARY *YÜEH-FU*

送別　　王維

下馬飲君酒
問君何不得之意
君言卧南山陲問時
歸臥莫復盡
但去無盡
白雲

TO SEE A FRIEND OFF *Wang Wei*

1.	down (dismount)	horse	drink	you	wine
2.	ask	you	where-not	to-	go
3.	you	say	not	happy (get-what-you-want)	
4.	return	lie	South	Hill	side
5.	but	go	do-not (imp.)	again	ask
6.	white	cloud/s	no	end	time

1. Dismount and drink this wine.
2. Where to? I ask.
3. At odds with the world:
4. Return to rest by the South Hill.
5. Go. Go. Do not ask again.
6. Endless, the white clouds.

桃源行　　王維

漁舟逐水愛山春，兩岸桃花夾古津。
坐看紅樹不知遠，行盡青溪不見人。
山口潛行始隈隩，山開曠望旋平陸。
遙看一處攢雲樹，近入千家散花竹。
樵客初傳漢姓名，居人未改秦衣服。
居人共住武陵源，還從物外起田園。
月明松下房櫳靜，日出雲中雞犬喧。
驚聞俗客爭來集，競引還家問都邑。

AFTER SOURCE OF THE PEACH
BLOSSOM STREAM
Wang Wei

Fishing boat driving water;
   loved mountains in spring.
Two banks of peach-blossoms
   lined the ancient source.
Red trees followed by red trees;
   hardly aware of distance.
End of the green stream:
   no person.
Skulked through a mountain opening,
   curving and swerving in.
Mountain opened up;
   view stretched—wide flat plain.
One spot in the distance,
   clusters of cloud-trees.
Nearing: thousands of houses,
   scattering flowers and bamboos.
Word from woodcutters:
   clan names of the Han Dynasty;
Residents' clothes
   still in the Ch'in styles.
Residents, living at
   source of Wu-ling stream,
Tilled fields and gardens
   beyond *this* world.
Bright moon. Beneath pines,
   latticed houses all quiet.
Sun up among clouds:
   cocks' crow, dogs' bark.
Surprise. Newcomer!
   people gathered and gathered,
And vying to be host, asked:

平明閭巷掃花開
薄暮漁樵乘水入
初因避地去人間
及至成仙遂不還
峽裡誰知有人事
世中遙望空雲山
不疑靈境難聞見
塵心未盡思鄉縣
出洞無論隔山水
辭家終擬長游衍
自謂經過舊不迷
安知峰壑今來變
當時只記入山深
青溪幾度到雲林
春來遍是桃花水
不辨仙源何處尋

how, such and such a town?
Dawn on streets and lanes:
   sweeping of flowers.
Dusk: fishermen and woodcutters,
   riding ripples home.
To escape execution,
   they first left men's world;
Then with this godliness:
   gone, thoughts of return.
At this gorge, who should care
   about men's affairs?
View from men's world:
   cloud-mountains, mountain-clouds.
"Once in a blue moon"
   never flashed upon him.
And dust-heart still stirring,
   thought of home still surging.
Out of cave: "No matter blocked
   by how many mountains and rivers,
I will leave home
   to live and roam there."
So sure that a road thus traversed
   would never be lost to him;
Yet valleys and peaks
   no longer the same valleys and peaks.
That time: only remembered
   deep deep into the mountain;
Green stream, many curves,
   then cloud-forests.
Spring comes: peach-blossom water
   flows everywhere.
Dustless garden, how to tell?
   where to find?

(written at the age of 19)

宣州謝朓樓餞別校書叔雲

李白

棄我去者昨日之日不可留

亂我心者今日之日多煩憂

長風萬里送秋雁

對此可以酣高樓

蓬萊文章建安骨

中間小謝又清發

俱懷逸興壯思飛

欲上青天攬明月

抽刀斷水水更流

舉杯消愁愁更愁

人生在世不稱意

明朝散髮弄扁舟

TO SEE SECRETARY SHU-YÜN OFF AT THE HSIEH T'IAO TOWER AT HSÜAN-CH'ENG *Li Po*

That which abandoned me—
Yesterday's day did not stay;
That which throws my heart in chaos—
Today's day, much too much sorrow.
Long winds, a million miles, see autumn geese away.
Facing this, I can drink and think, up in the high tower:
Literature of P'eng-lai, style of Chien-an poets.
Also the lesser Hsieh who came out limpid and fresh.
All cherish free-flowing expressions and high-flown thoughts.
Wanting to scale the sky to hold the moon.
I take my sword to cut the water: water still flows.
I hold up my drink to quench my sorrow: sorrow, sorrow still goes.
Man living in this world is always at odds with it:
Tomorrow morning: unloose our hair and go a-boating.

古風第六　　　　李白

越燕習狀闕前日天鵾翔賞宣將邊
思戀所其門庭海胡虜雖不可飛三
不不有固雁亂迷生逐功難李沒
馬禽性風別戍沙雪蠱魂戰誠悽百
代越情土昔今鶩飛蟻心苦忠誰自

KU FENG (AFTER THE STYLE OF ANCIENT POEMS)
NO. 6 *Li Po*

1. Tai	horse	not	think	Yüeh
2. Yüeh	fowl	not	love	Yen
3. feeling	nature	have	(what)	accustom
4. folk	custom manners	deep-to naturally	its	the-way-things-used-to-be-like
5. previously	leave	Yen	Men	Pass
6. now	stationed	Dragon	Court	front
7. startling	sand	derange confound	sea-	sun (i.e., sun above the "Vast Sea," ancient name for the Mongolian Desert)
8. flying	snow	bewilder	Tartar	sky
9. lice	—	grow	tiger-	fighter-pheasant (i.e., helmets and mails)
10. heart	soul	chase	feather-flag	silk-banner
11. bitter	fight	merit	not	rewarded
12. loyalty	sincerity	difficult	to	publicize express
13. who	take-pity-on	Li	Flying	General
14. white	head	die disappear	three	borders

1. North-born horses do not think of Yüeh in the south.
2. Fowls of Yüeh do not love Yen, the north region.
3. Nature and feeling are born of habit.
4. Likewise, native manners.
5. We took leave at the Wild-goose Pass,
6. And are now garrisoned at the Dragon-Court.
7. Startling sand confounds the sun above the "Vast Sea."*
8. Flying snow bewilders the barbarian sky.
9. Lice grow inside helmets and mails.
10. Our spirit is driven with the silken banners.
11. Hard fight earns no imperial reward.
12. Loyalty is difficult to express.
13. Who would pity the Winged General Li,
14. Who, white-headed, was lost among the border states?†

---

*The Vast Sea (*han-hai*) is the ancient name for the Mongolian Desert, so named because "the sand flies like waves and people and horses are lost in it as if sinking."
†Li Kuang, died 125 B.C.

古風第十四　　　　李白

沙古黃虜漢堵霜骸虐武皇鼓氣土人雨
風終草戎大遺千榛陵威聖聲殺中萬如
饒竟秋望空無橫骸誰毒我事變騷六淒
闕索落高城邑骨峨閒驕怒師和卒十哀
胡蕭木登荒邊白嵯借天赫勞陽發三哀

1.	Tartar barbarian	pass	abound-in	wind/s	sand/s
2.	bleak	lifeless	last (v.)	ancient	—
3.	tree/s	fall	autumn	grass	yellow
4.	ascend	high	watch	western (barbarians)	enemy
5.	deserted	castle	empty	vast	desert
6.	side	village	not	left-behind remaining	wall
7.	white	bone/s	lie-across	thousand (i.e., a thousand year)	frost
8.	abrupt (i.e., the towering look of mountains)	—	cover	hazel	grove
9.	by means of (i.e., ask of others)	ask	who	oppress	maltreat
10.	heaven (i.e., the Huns)	pride	malicious	martial	warlikeness
11.	awful(ly) outrageous-(ly)	angry anger	our	holy	emperor
12.	labor	army military-power	employ	war-drums	—
13.	the principle of *Yang* (i.e., the active, positive)	harmony	change	killing	air
14.	dispatch	soldiers	disturb sadden	middle (middle Kingdom)	land
15.	three-hundred-and-sixty-thousand		—	men	
16.	sorrowful	sorrowful	tear/s	like	rain/s

役圃兒苦在庖
行農戍山不尉
就營征鬭今飼
悲得見知牧人
且安不豈李邊

258

17.	at-the-same-time	sad	proceed	expedition	—
18.	how	can	take-care-of	farm	garden
19.	not	see	expeditionary (frontier men)	—	son/s
20.	how	know	pass	mountain	bitterness
21.	Li	Mu	now	not	present
22.	border frontier	men	feed	wolf/ves	tiger/s

1. The barbarian pass is filled with windblown sand
2. Squalling from ancient times till now.
3. Trees stripped of leaves, autumn grass go yellow.
4. We climb up to look over the barbarous land:
5. Desolate castle, vast empty desert,
6. No wall left to this frontier village,
7. White bones lying across a thousand frosts,
8. Huge mounds, covered by thorns and brushwoods.
9. Who is the aggressor? Let me ask.
10. The barbarians' malicious martial move
11. Has brought the emperor's flaming anger.
12. He ordered the army to beat the war-drums.
13. Calm sun turned into murderous air.
14. He called for soldiers, causing a turmoil over the Middle Kingdom.
15. Three hundred and sixty thousand men.
16. Sorrow, sorrow, tears like rain.
17. Grief-drenched, yet we had to go.
18. How are we to farm our fields?
19. Without seeing the frontier men
20. Who would know the dreary sorrow at the pass?
21. General Li Mu is no longer there.
22. We guardsmen fed to tigers and wolves.

李　白

八
時李花水水流人遊動侯陽樓日州龍頭易丘堂羞舞謳

十月與腸流後續舊上色公上城雲皇飛馬辟嵩高珍趙逩

第三桃斷東後相非橋海羅西半照散如絡皆橫上錯引隨

風津門馬逐水今人年鳴帝洛輝冠下馬金人氣門鼎風管

古天千朝暮前古新年雞謁月餘衣朝鞍黃行志入列香清

1. T'ien	Tsin	third	month	time
2. thousand	gate	peach/es	and	plum/s
3. morning	as	break (i.e., heart-breaking)	intestines	flower/s
4. evening	chase	eastward	flowing	water
5. front	water	again	hind	water
6. ancient	present	after-each-other	continue	flow
7. new/today	man	not	old	man
8. year	year	bridge	on	tour; roam
9. rooster	crow	sea	color	move
10. to-have-an-audience-of	emperor	place-in-order	noblemen	—
11. moon	fall	western	Shang (the name of a palace)	Yang
12. remaining	ray	half	castle	tower
13. rob/s	cap/s	shine	cloud	sun
14. levee	down	scatter	imperial	capital
15. saddle	horse/s	like	flying	dragon/s
16. yellow	gold	halter	horse	head
17. pedestrian/s	—	all	avoid (i.e., evict)	change
18. ambition	—	cross	Sung	Mountain
19. enter	gate	ascend	high	hall/s
20. lined	caldron	mix	treasured	food
21. fragrant	wind	usher-in	Chao	dance
22. clear	pipe/s	follow	Ch'i	song/s

七雙行自功自黃綠何散
十雙樂言成古犬珠如髮
紫戲爭度身多空成鴇棹
駕庭晝千不悠歡費夷扁
鴛幽夜秋退尤息譬子舟

23.	seventy	—	purple	mandarin-ducks	—
24.	pair	pair	play	yard	shade
25.	practice (i.e., entertain oneself)	pleasure	strive	day	night
26.	self	say	pass	thousand	autumn/s
27.	merit distinction	achieve	body person	not	retreat retire
28.	since	ancient	plenty	mistake/s	—
29.	yellow	dog	vainly	sigh	—
30.	Green	Pearl	become	challenge	feud
31.	how	like	Ti (i.e., Fan-li)	Yi	Tzu
32.	loosen	hair	row	small	boat

1. The third month in T'ientsin:
2. A thousand gates of peach and plum trees;
3. In the morning, heart-smiting flowers.
4. In the evening, they drift with eastward water.
5. Water gone and water coming on,
6. Flow, flow from ancient days till now.

7. Today's men are not those of yesterday.
8. Year after year they hang around on the bridge.
9. Cocks crow. Sea sheen stirs.
10. At levee, princes spread in order.
11. The moon falls beyond West Shang-yang Palace.
12. Receding light catches half the wall-towers.
13. Robes and caps shine against the cloud and sun.
14. Levee over, they disperse from the Capital.
15. Saddled horses are like flying dragons,
16. Gold trappings over their heads.
17. Street-people flee in all directions.
18. Haughty indeed, these men's will across the highest peak.
19. Enter doors. Ascend imposing halls.
20. Caldrons with mixed rare food spread out.
21. Fragrant winds usher in the dancing.
22. Clear pipes follow spirited singing.
23. Seventy purple ducks and drakes,
24. Pair by pair, play in the dark of the court,
25. Strive to make merry day and night,
26. And pass a thousand autumns, they say.
27. Mission accomplished, to stay on
28. Means, in history, a greater downfall.
29. Li Ssu, at death, sighed over his yellow dog.[1]
30. Lady Lü-chu's beauty triggered tragic rivalry.[2]
31. None can compare to Fan-li[3]
32. Who loosened his hair and went a-boating.

[1] Li Ssu, a prime minister in the Ch'in Dynasty, fell from grace and was to be executed in the capital. On the way he remarked to his son, "I wish I could bring our yellow dog and go rabbitting with you again!" At that, they both wept. (From *Shih-chi*)

[2] This line refers to the story of Lü Chu recorded in the biography of Shih Ch'ung (249–300). Lü Chu, Green Pearl, is Shih's most beloved concubine. Sun Hsiu, a high-ranking official, sued for her. Shih refused him. Sun made false mandates to execute Shih. "Now I shall be executed on account of you," said Shih to Lü Chu who wept and replied, "It is fit for me to die before you" and jumped down from the top storey to death.

[3] Fan-li, after having succeeded in helping the king of Yüeh to overthrow the king of Wu, retreated from public life.

江上吟　　李白

木蘭之枻沙棠舟
玉簫金管坐兩頭
美酒樽中置千斛
載妓隨波任去留
仙人有待乘黃鶴
海客無心隨白鷗
屈平詞賦懸日月
楚王臺榭空山丘
興酣落筆搖五嶽
詩成笑傲凌滄洲
功名富貴若長在
漢水亦應西北流

RIVER SONG *Li Po*

1.	magnolia	—	's	oar/s	spice-wood	—	boat
2.	jade	flute	gold	pipe/s	sit	two	ends
3.	beautiful	wine	bottle	middle	store	thousand	pecks
4.	carry	girl-entertainer	follow	wave/s	allow	going	staying
5.	immortal	—	yet-to-wait	—	ride	yellow	crane
6.	sea	traveller	no	mind	follow	white	seagull/s
7.	Ch'ü P'ing (i.e., Ch'ü Yüan)		poetry	—	hang	sun	moon
8.	Ch'u	King	terrace	—	empty	mountain	hill
9.	impulse inspiration	full intoxicated enrapt	make-fall (i.e., apply)	pen	shake	Five	Peaks
10.	poem	finished	laughing	proud	rise-above	Ch'ang (i.e., the hermit's land)	Chou
11.	rank	fame	wealth	distinction	if	long	exist
12.	Han	River	also	should	west	north (i.e., flow northwestward)	flow

1. Magnolia oars; a boat of spice-wood.
2. Jade flutes, gold pipes; musicians fill stern and prow.
3. Bottles of fine wine measuring thousands of pecks.
4. With us are girls; we let loose on drifting waves.
5. A Taoist immortal waits for a yellow crane to take flight.
6. A seafarer, willy-nilly, follows the white gulls.
7. Ch'ü Yüan's songs hang with the sun and moon.
8. King Ch'u's terraces are all barren hills now.
9. High-spirited, I hold pen and shake the Five Peaks.
10. Poem done, I laugh and ride above the Blue Coves.*
11. If name and rank could last forever,
12. The Han River would be northwestward bound.

*A kind of fairyland for people who decide to live in seclusion.

侍從宜春苑奉詔賦龍池柳色初青聽新鶯百囀歌

李白

東風已綠瀛洲草，紫殿紅樓覺春好。
池南柳色半青青，縈煙裊娜拂綺城。
垂絲百尺掛雕楹，上有好鳥相和鳴。
間關早得春風情，春風卷入碧雲去，
千門萬戶皆春聲。是時君王在鎬京，
五雲垂暉耀紫清。仗出金宮隨日轉，
天回玉輦繞花行。始向蓬萊看舞鶴，
還過茝若聽新鶯。新鶯飛繞上林苑，
願入簫韶雜鳳笙。

POEM COMPOSED AT THE COMMAND OF THE EMPEROR IN I-CHUN PARK ON THE DRAGON-POND AS THE WILLOWS ARE IN THEIR FRESH GREEN AND THE NEW ORIOLES ARE SINGING IN THEIR THOUSAND WAYS *Li Po*

1. east	wind/s	already	make-green	Ying	Chou	grass
2. purple	palace/s hall/s	red	tower/s	feel	spring	good
3. pond	south	willow	color shade	half	green	green
4. reeling	smoke	slender	graceful	flap	brocade multi-colored	city
5. dangling	tassel/s	hundred	feet	hanging	carved	column
6. above	there-is	good fair	bird	with-each-other	harmonize	cry
7. chien (onomatopoeic)	kuan	early	get	spring	wind/s	feeling
8. spring	wind/s	roll	enter	blue	cloud/s	go
9. thousand	door/s	ten-thousand	gate/s	all	spring	sound
10. that	time	emperor	—	in	Hao	Capital
11. five	cloud/s	hang let-down	ray	shine	purple (i.e., sky)	blue
12. insignia retinue	leave	gold	palace	follow	"sun"	turn
13. "sky"	turn	jade	imperial carriage	around	flower/s	walk
14. first	toward	P'eng	Lai	watch	dancing	crane/s
15. then	pass	Chih	Shih	listen-to	new	oriole/s
16. new	oriole/s	fly	encircle	Shang	Lin	Park
17. wish	enter	Shun's music	—	mix	phoenix-pipe/s	—

1. East winds have blown the grass green in Ying-chou.
2. Purple halls, red towers: feel the fine spring day.
3. South of the pool, willows' color is half-green.
4. Reeling smoke, graceful curls, flap the brocade city.
5. Tassel-branches, a hundred feet, dangle about carved columns.
6. And above, nice birds sing to each other:
7. "Kuan, kuan"—the first to get the feel of spring winds.
8. Spring winds roll themselves into the blue clouds.
9. A thousand doors, a million houses, brim with spring voices.
10. The Emperor is now at Capital Hao.*
11. Five Clouds pour rays and brighten the Purple Sky.
12. Insignia issue from the golden palace and turn with the "Sun."
13. The "Sky" turns the jade phaeton around the flowers.
14. He goes first to Penglai to see cranes dance
15. And then returns to Chih-shih to listen to new orioles
16. The new orioles circle above the Shang-lin Park†
17. Longing to plunge into the music and mix with the phoenix-pipes.

*This refers to the capital of Kings Wen and Wu of Chou Dynasty (i.e., model rulers).
†A reference to the court life described in Ssu-ma Hsiang-ju's (179–117 B.C.) "The Shang-lin Park," hence to courting with the emperor.

    Other conventional phrases mean: Five Clouds = auspicious breath = the imperial influences on man and nature. Purple Sky = dwelling of the celestial emperor. Sun = emperor. Sky = emperor.

憶舊遊寄譙郡元參軍　李白

憶昔洛陽董糟丘
為余天津橋南造酒樓
黃金白璧買歌笑
一醉累月輕王侯
海內賢豪青雲客
就中與君心莫逆
迴山轉海不作難
傾情倒意無所惜
我向淮南攀桂枝
君留洛北愁夢思
不忍別
還相隨
相隨迢迢訪仙城
三十六曲水回縈
一溪初入千花明
萬壑度盡松風聲
銀鞍金絡到平地
漢東太守來相迎
紫陽之真人

樂鳴舉舞身股霄朝遥巢橋虎虜行苦深金案心曲玉

仙鳳輕起我其九終水故渭貌戎太腸月黃玉歸西碧

笙動驚欲醉覆枕氣凌不山尋波勇過度羊歲輕青無城如

玉上似催守袍眠意欲闕山家君州呼道涼義食鮑向水

吹樓宛管太錦橫意兩楚還歸巖並相不北貴綺醉出流

我霞然長中持醉筵雜飛既亦家尹月輪來君杯我時祠

邀餐嚼神漢手我富星分余君君作五摧行感瓊使時晋

鳴緣過何日娥輝衣去飛遇賦期去君群少紛紛辭憶

鼓草經雪斜翠月羅空再楊可歸遇離多紛此相

簫莎惢似宜窩初舞入行難長不還一又今爭盡極緘遙

水鱗妓花醉渾娟唱歌繞樂獻雲首頭北此恨暮可可跂里

弄龍攜楊歌清嬋更吹自行因青自南之別春不不長千

舟波来若妝尺娥人風曲時遊關山橋臺余花亦亦兒君

浮微興其紅百翠美清歌此西北東渭鄞問落言情吟寄

271

REMEMBERING OUR EXCURSION IN THE PAST:
A LETTER SENT TO COMMISSARY YEN OF
CH'AO COUNTY *Li Po*

1. I remembered Tung Tsao-chiu of Lo-yang
2. Who once built me a wine-shop south of T'ientsin Bridge.
3. Yellow gold, white jade to buy songs and laughter.
4. Drunk for months on end; in our eyes, no king, no lord.
5. Among cloud-riding worthies and heroes all over the world
6. With you I was most in tune.
7. To us, mountain-crossing and sea-crossing meant nothing,
8. Our hearts and minds were open: nothing to hold back.
9. I went south of Huai River to clamber along laurel boughs.
10. You stayed north of Lo, dreaming, thinking, sad.
11. Wanting no separation,
12. We came together.
13. Together to visit the removed City of Immortals.
14. Thirty-six turns of whirling and winding water.
15. Entering—a stream of a thousand bright flowers.
16. Millions of valleys we passed; surges of pine-winds.
17. Horses with silver saddles and gold trappings arrived at level ground.
18. The magistrate of East Han came to meet us.
19. The "True Man" of Tzu-yang
20. Invited me to play the jade flute.
21. On the Tower of Feasting Mist celestial music stirred,
22. Blending, echoing like phoenix cries.
23. Long sleeves, touched by the flutes, tended to rise.
24. The magistrate of Middle Han, now drunk, began to dance,
25. His hand holding a brocade robe to cover me.
26. Drunk, I wanted to sleep and pillowed on his thigh,
27. At the banquet our spirit soared beyond the nine skies,
28. Stars parted, rain scattered before the morning came.
29. Into different directions from Ch'u, over distant mountains and rivers.
30. I went back myself to the mountains, my old nest.
31. And you returned home, crossing the Wei Bridge.
32. Your father, brave like a leopard or tiger,
33. Then governor of *Ping* to halt barbarians,
34. Called me in May to cross the T'ai-heng ranges.
35. Broken wheels, I don't have to say, over sheep-gut roads
36. And late in the year arrived at Liang in the north,
37. Moved at your weighing friendship over gold.
38. Jade cups, rich dishes on emerald trays

39. Made me drunk, food-full, no more thoughts of returning home.
40. Often we went out west of the City to the bend
41. Around the Chin Temple where there was a river like green jade.
42. Float a boat; stir the water; flutes and drums joined.
43. A little wave; dragon scales; cyperaceous green.
44. On impulse, we brought girls and drifted to and fro.
45. They were like catkins, or rather, flakes of snow.
46. Rouge makeup, like drunkenness, to go with the sunset.
47. On the green water, a hundred feet deep, were written the eyebrows.
48. Green eyebrows, fair and refined; bright, cresent-bright.
49. Beautiful girls sang in turn, as the brocade swirled into dance.
50. Clear winds blew the songs into the sky,
51. And the songs flew around the clouds.
52. Such a moment, such pleasure, was difficult to have again.
53. I went west to offer "Rhymeprose of the Long Willow"
54. Blue-cloud fame in the court was unattained.
55. To East Ranges; white-headed, I returned
56. And met you again south of Bridge of Wei.
57. North of Chan, we made separation.
58. You asked me how much sadness I know:
59. Falling flowers at spring dusk bustle in confusion.
60. To talk about it? There is no end.
61. To spell my emotion? There is no word.
62. I call my son to kneel down and seal this letter
63. And send it to you, a thousand miles, and thinking.

李白

行

窈劇來梅里猜婦開壁回眉厌信臺行堆䯀哀跡苔掃

覆前馬青干嫌君嘗晴一展與柱夫遠預可上行綠能

干初門竹弄長無爲未向不始塵抱望君灩不天舊生不

髮花騎牀居小四顏頭喚五同存上六塘月聲前一深

長妾折郎遠同兩十羞低千十願常豈十瞿五猿門一苔

274

THE SONG OF CH'ANG-KAN (*YÜEH-FU*) *Li Po*

1.	concubine (i.e., my, humble term used by women when speaking of themselves)	hair	first	cover	forehead
2.	pluck	flower/s	door	front	play
3.	you	ride	bamboo	horse	come
4.	circling circle	bed	play	green	plum/s
5.	together	live	Ch'ang	Kan	village prefecture
6.	two	small	no	hate	suspicion
7.	fourteen	—	be	your	wife
8.	shy	face	has-never	—	open
9.	lower	head	face	dark	wall
10.	thousand	call/s	not	one once	turn look-back
11.	fifteen	—	then begin	unknit	brows
12.	wish	together	dust	and	ashes
13.	often	keep-in-mind	embrace	pillar	reliability trustwor-thiness
14.	how	ascend	Watch	Husband	Terrace
15.	sixteen	—	you	a-long-way	go
16.	Ch'ü	T'ang	Yen	Yü	pile-of-rocks (in the midst of river)
17.	fifth	month	cannot	—	offend touch
18.	ape	sound	heaven	above	sorrowful
19.	door	front	late	departure	foot-step/s
20.	each-one	—	grow	green	moss
21.	moss	deep	cannot	—	sweep

落　葉　秋　風　早
八　月　蝴　蜨　来
雙　飛　西　園　草
感　此　傷　妻　心
坐　愁　紅　顔　老
早　晩　下　三　巴
預　將　書　報　家
相　迎　不　道　遠
直　至　長　風　沙

22.	falling	leaf	autumn	wind/s	early
23.	eighth	month	butterflies	—	come
24.	pair	fly	west	garden	grass
25.	moved-by	this	hurt	my	heart
26.	sit	grieve	red	face	old
27.	soon	late	down	three (i.e., Three Gorges)	Pa's
28.	in-advance	(part.)	letter	inform	home
29.	(each-other)	welcome	not	say	far
30.	all-the-way-to	—	Long	Wind	Sand

1. My hair barely covered my forehead.
2. I played in front of the gate, plucking flowers.
3. You came riding on a bamboo-horse.
4. And around the bed we played with green plums.
5. We were then living in Ch'ang-kan.
6. Two small people, no hate nor suspicion.
7. At fourteen, I became your wife.
8. I seldom laughed, being bashful.
9. I lowered my head toward the dark wall.
10. Called to, a thousand times, I never looked back.
11. At fifteen, I began to perk up.
12. We wished to stay together like dust and ash.
13. If you have the faith of Wei-sheng.*
14. Why do I have to climb up the waiting tower?
15. At sixteen, you went on a long journey.
16. By the Yen-jü rocks at Ch'ü-t'ang
17. The unpassable rapids in the fifth month
18. When monkeys cried against the sky.
19. Before the door your footprints
20. Are all moss-grown
21. Moss too deep to sweep away.
22. Falling leaves: autumn winds are early.
23. In the eighth month, butterflies come
24. In pairs over the grass in the West Garden.
25. These smite my heart.
26. I sit down worrying and youth passes away.
27. When eventually you would come down from the Three Gorges.
28. Please let me know ahead of time.
29. I will meet you, no matter how far,
30. Even all the way to Long Wind Sand.

*Wei-sheng had a date with a girl at a pillar under the bridge. The girl did not show up. The water came. He died holding tight at the pillar. (From *Shih Chi*)
    The waiting tower in the next line, literally, is wait-for-husband tower or rock which alludes to a story of a woman waiting for the return of her husband on a Hill. One version has it that she was turned into a rock while waiting.

玉 階 怨　　　　李 白

玉 階 生 白 露
夜 久 侵 羅 襪
卻 下 水 精 簾
玲 瓏 望 秋 月

YÜ CHIEH YÜAN (JADE STEPS GRIEVANCE, YÜEH-FU)* *Li Po*

1.	jade	step/s	grow	white	dew
2.	night	late	soak; attack	gauze	stocking/s
3.	let-	down	crystal	—	blind
4.	glass-clear	—	watch	autumn	moon

1. Upon the jade steps white dews grow.
2. It is late. Gauze stockings are dabbled.
3. She lets down the crystal blind
4. To watch, glass-clear, the autumn moon.

*Also classified as *wu-chüeh*. One of the earliest models of this poem is a *yüeh-fu* of the same title by Hsieh T'iao (464–499), a poet Li Po greatly admired.

望嶽　　　　杜甫

岱宗夫如何　齊魯青未了
造化鍾神秀　陰陽割昏曉
盪胸生曾雲　決眥入歸鳥
會當凌絕頂　一覽眾山小

LOOKING AT MOUNT T'AI-SHAN *Tu Fu*

1.	Tai (i.e., T'ai-shan)	Tsung	(part.)	how	—
2.	Ch'i	Lu	green	not-yet	over
3.	Creation	—	concentrate	miraculous	beauty
4.	Yin	Yang	cut	dusk	dawn
5.	turbulent	breast	grow	layered	cloud/s
6.	force	eyelid	enter	return	bird/s
7.	expect	should	exceed	extreme	summit
8.	one	glance	various	mountains	small

1. How about the Mount of Mounts?
2. From Ch'i to Lu, never ending green.
3. Great Transformation centers here divine beauty.
4. Shade and light divides here dusk and dawn.
5. Rolling chest: in it are born layers of clouds.
6. Eyelids strained to open by incoming birds from afar.
7. Ah! to stand atop the highest peak
8. To see: how tiny the rest of the hills!

兵車行　　杜甫

車轔轔　馬蕭蕭　行人弓箭各在腰

耶孃妻子走相送　塵埃不見咸陽橋

牽衣頓足攔道哭　哭聲直上干雲霄

道旁過者問行人　行人但云點行頻

或從十五北防河　便至四十西營田

去時里正與裹頭　歸來頭白還戍邊

邊庭流血成海水　武皇開邊意未已

君不聞　漢家山東二百州　千村萬落生荊杞

SONG OF THE WAR-CHARIOTS (YÜEH-FU) *Tu Fu*

1. War-chariots rumble.
2. Horses neigh.
3. People on the road, arrows and bows at their belts.
4. Fathers, mothers, wives, children rush to see them off.
5. Dust rises: the Hsien-yang Bridge cannot be seen.
6. Pulling at clothes, stamping feet, blocking roads and weeping,
7. Weeping reaches straight to the skies beyond clouds.
8. Passersby ask them why.
9. They say: constant conscription.
10. At fifteen: go north to defend the River.
11. At forty: west to cultivate camp-fields.
12. Going: district leaders turban their heads.
13. Returning: white-headed, still to guard the frontier.
14. At the frontier, blood flows like the sea.
15. Emperor Wu is still hot at extending the borders.
16. Do you not see, upon the two thousand districts east of Hua Shan,
17. A thousand hamlets, a million villages, all thorn-grown?

縱有健婦把鋤犁，禾生隴畝無東西。
況復秦兵耐苦戰，被驅不異犬與雞。
長者雖有問，役夫敢申恨？
且如今年冬，未休關西卒。
縣官急索租，租稅從何出？
信知生男惡，反是生女好。
生女猶得嫁比鄰，生男埋沒隨百草。
君不見，青海頭，古來白骨無人收。
新鬼煩冤舊鬼哭，天陰雨濕聲啾啾。

18. Strong women there may be to hoe and plow,
19. Plants overgrow furrows, what east, what west?
20. And soldiers at the Passes, all hard fighters,
21. Are driven along like chickens and dogs.
22. The elders may sometimes ask,
23. Do they dare complain?
24. Now take this winter:
25. Frontier guards still on duty west of the Pass,
26. District officers should fiercely demand taxes and rent!
27. Taxes and rent! where to obtain?
28. To have a son is cursed.
29. To have a daughter is, oddly, better.
30. A daughter can be married to a neighboring house.
31. A son is doomed to be buried among weeds.
32. Do you not see, near the Kokonor shores,
33. Since ancient times white bones exposed to sun and rain?
34. New ghosts complain, old ghosts wail.
35. Darkening sky, drizzling rains, there *swish-swish* all too sad!

杜甫

夢李白二首

死別已吞聲，生別常惻惻。
江南瘴癘地，逐客無消息。
故人入我夢，明我長相憶。
恐非平生魂，路遠不可測。
魂來楓林青，魂返關塞黑。
君今在羅網，何以有羽翼。
落月滿屋梁，猶疑照顏色。
水深波浪闊，無使蛟龍得。

DREAMING OF LI PO *Tu Fu*

I

1. Death separation: sobs hard to swallow.
2. Life separation: grief daily strikes.
3. South of the Yangtze, land of miasma,
4. No news of my exiled friend!
5. My friend enters my dream
6. Knowing that of him I often think.
7. Is it that you are no live soul?—
8. Covering such distance! Immeasurable!
9. Soul comes: maples flicker green.
10. Soul goes: all the Passes darken.
11. You were caught in nets.
12. How now you come in wings?
13. Full moon falls upon the beam,
14. Suspicious light, doubtful sheen!
15. Deep water, high-rising waves.
16. Don't let the serpent pull you in!

行至君意促易波墜首志華悴恢累名事
日不夢君局不風失白生京憔恢反歲後
終久頻見常来多恐搔平滿獨網身萬身
雲子夜親歸道湖楫門負蓋人云老秋寞
浮游三情苦苦江舟出若冠斯孰將午寂

II

17. Floating clouds travel all day long.
18. The wanderer has not returned.
19. Three nights on end I dreamt of you.
20. Such affection you have shown.
21. Always in haste you said: I'm going.
22. Sorrowfully you said: "Difficult to come!
23. High waves upon seas and rivers!
24. And fear falling off from the boat!"
25. Out of the gate, you scratched your white hair
26. As if burdened by your whole life's will.
27. Successful officials all over the Capital.
28. You alone are pressed and depressed.
29. Who says the meshes of Justice are wide?
30. Aging like this, you got involved.
31. Name for a thousand a million years?
32. After this body is gone, lonely only lonely . . .

琵琶行　　　白居易

潯陽江頭夜送客　楓葉荻花秋瑟瑟
主人下馬客在船　舉酒欲飲無管絃
醉不成歡慘將別　別時茫茫江浸月
忽聞水上琵琶聲　主人忘歸客不發
尋聲暗問彈者誰　琵琶聲停欲語遲
移船相近邀相見　添酒回燈重開宴
千呼萬喚始出來　猶抱琵琶半遮面
轉軸撥絃三兩聲　未成曲調先有聲

SONG OF THE P'I-P'A (WITH INTRODUCTION)
Po Chü-i (772–846)

*In the tenth year of Yüan-ho (815), I was banished to Chiu-chiang
County to be an assistant official there. In the autumn of the second year,
I was seeing a friend off at Pen-pu at night when I heard someone play
the p'i-p'a with the touch and style of the Capital. I asked about the
player and found that she was from Ch'ang-an and was once a student
of Masters Mu and Ts'ao. Aging, her beauty declining, she married her-
self to a merchant. I ordered to have wine and food again and asked her
to play a few tunes. Afterward, she looked sad and started telling us
about the happy days of her youth and how she now became haggard,
drifting along rivers and lakes. It is now two years since I left the court to
come here. I have felt content until tonight when her words made me re-
alize the very meaning of my banishment. I wrote this long poem of
eighty-eight lines for her and titled it "Song of the P'i-p'a."*

I went to Hsün-yang River to see a friend off at night.
Maple leaves, flowering rushes whistled with autumn.
I dismounted. My guest was inside the boat.
We raised our drink, sad to find no music.
Drunk without ending in joy! then, separation!
Separation: blurring river soaked the moon.

似訴平生不得志
低眉信手續續彈
說盡心中無限事
輕攏慢撚抹復挑
初為霓裳後六么
大弦嘈嘈如急雨
小弦切切如私語
嘈嘈切切錯雜彈
大珠小珠落玉盤
閒關鶯語花底滑
幽咽泉流冰下難
冰泉冷澀弦凝絕
凝絕不通聲暫歇
別有幽愁暗恨生
此時無聲勝有聲
銀瓶乍破水漿迸
鐵騎突出刀槍鳴
曲終收撥當心畫

Suddenly, I heard strings of a *p'i-p'a* across the water.
I forgot to return. My guest held his boat.
We followed the music in the dark asking for the player.
The *p'i-p'a* stopped. It took her sometime to answer.
We moved our boat closer and invited her over.
"More wine!" "Lights again!" "Spread the table!"
A thousand calls, a million applauses, she then came out,
Still half-covering her face with her *p'i-p'a*.
Merely turning the pegs, strumming once or twice,
Melody hardly formed, her feeling already swelled.
Each string, a muffling note; each sound, a thought,
As if to pour out her whole life's odds.
She lowered her brows, plucking along off and on,
Telling the immeasurable matters of her heart.
Light brushes, slow presses and then picking.
First, the *Rainbow Skirt*, then, the *Green Waist*.
Large strings, *shaft-shaft*, like sudden rains.
Small strings, *chat-chat*, like whispering.
Shaft-shaft, chat-chat, mixing and merging.

四絃一聲如裂帛
東船西舫悄無言
唯見江心秋月白
沈吟放撥插絃中
整頓衣裳起斂容
自言本是京城女
家在蝦蟆陵下住
十三學得琵琶成
名屬教坊第一部
曲罷曾教善才服
妝成每被秋娘妒
五陵年少爭纏頭
一曲紅綃不知數
鈿頭銀篦擊節碎
血色羅裙翻酒污
今年歡笑復明年
秋月春風等閒度
弟走從軍阿姨死

Large pearls, small pearls poured into a jade tray.
Kuan-kuan, the orioles glided beneath the flowers.
Swallowed sobs, the fountain sped down the beach.
Fountain water, cutting cold: strings seem to clod, breaking off.
Clodding, breaking, blocked, sound suddenly stilled
As a fresh kind of grief and grievance darkly grew.
This minute, silence won over sound.
A silver bottle brusquely broken: liquid gushed all over.
Armored horses came out of ambush: jingling swords and sabres.
The song ended with a fast brush toward the heart.
Four strings, one sound, like tearing silk.
East boat, west boat, all quiet.
Only in the middle of the river: one white autumn moon.
Murmuring, she put the pick back among the strings.
She straightened her clothes and composed herself
And said, "I came from the Capital
And lived near the Mount of Hsia-ma.
At thirteen, I mastered the art of the *p'i-p'a*,
Ranking first among my peers in the workshop.
Every tune I played stunned even experts.
My beauty, the object of envy for all the girls.

暮去朝來顏色故
門前冷落鞍馬稀
老大嫁作商人婦
商人重利輕別離
前月浮梁買茶去
去來江口守空船
繞船月明江水寒
夜深忽夢少年事
夢啼妝淚紅闌干
我聞琵琶已嘆息
又聞此語重唧唧
同是天涯淪落人
相逢何必曾相識
我從去年辭帝京
謫居臥病潯陽城
潯陽地僻無音樂
終歲不聞絲竹聲
住近湓江地低濕

Noble youths from Wu-ling poured in with gifts.
One song: uncountable rolls of red silk.
Gold combs, silver pins smashed in excited rhythm.
Skirts of dazzling blood-red stained in overturned wine.
This year, next year, merriment went on.
Autumn moons, spring winds passed to no end.
Then, my brother went to war, my aunt died.
Dusk went. Morning came. Colors changed.
At the door: cold! hardly any visit of carts and horses!
Aging, I became wife to a merchant
Who aimed for money first, cared little about separation.
He went to Fu-liang to buy tea last month,
Leaving me in an empty boat at the river's mouth.
All around my boat, bright moon and cold water.
In the deep night, I suddenly dreamt of days of youth
And woke in tears streaking all over my rouged face."
With her music I started to sigh.
Her story now shot my heart with more grief.
"We are both drifters across the world.
We meet. We feel. Do we need to know each other?
I took leave of the Capital last year,
Now an exile, often sick, at Hsün-yang.

生物鳴夜傾笛聽語明曲行立急聲泣多濕
宅何哀月獨村而琵斯一琶久轉前掩最衫
繞聞猿秋還與難琵耳彈琵良絃向皆誰青
竹暮血朝酒歌唧君樂坐作言似聞下馬
苦日啼花取山嘲聞仙更翻此促不重泣句
蘆聞鶘江往無啞夜聽辭君我坐凄座中州
黃其杜春往豈嘔今如莫爲感却凄滿座江

Hsün-yang, cut off from things, has no music.
All year round, no strings, no pipes.
My residence near Pen River is low and damp.
Yellow reeds, bitter bamboos encircle my house.
Morning till dusk: what do I hear?
But nightjars crying out their hearts and monkeys' howl.
Spring rivers, flowered mornings, autumn-moon nights,
I give myself to the cup and drink alone.
Mountain ballads, village pipes there are,
Crude, cacaphonous, hardly pleasing to the ear.
Tonight, the speech and song of your *p'i-p'a*
Is like celestial music clearing my ear.
Please don't go. Sit down. Play another tune.
I would like to write a lyric to your music."
Moved by my request, she stood for a while,
Sat down to her strings and strings quickened.
Sad, sad, no longer soaring like the previous tune.
All listeners there sobbed and wept.
Who among them has shed the most tears?
This official whose blue robe is now all drenched!

秋曉行南谷經荒村　柳宗元

杪秋霜露重
晨起行幽谷
黃葉覆溪橋
荒村唯古木
寒花疏寂歷
幽泉微斷續
機心久已忘
何事驚麋鹿

MORNING WALK IN AUTUMN TO SOUTH VALLEY
PASSING AN ABANDONED VILLAGE   *Liu Tsung-yüan*

1. tip	autumn	frost	dew	heavy
2. morning	rise	walk	secluded	valley
3. yellow	leaves	cover	stream	bridge
4. deserted	village	only	ancient	tree/s
5. cold	flower/s	sparse	quiet	—
6. sccluded	fountain	a-little	broken	connect
7. scheme	mind	longtime	already	forgotten
8. what	matter	startle	young-	deer

1. Autumn's end: frost and dew become heavy.
2. Get up early. Walk in secluded ravine.
3. Yellow leaves cover stream and bridge.
4. Deserted village: only ancient trees.
5. Cold flowers, sparse: quiet, alone.
6. Secluded spring, a little: heard, unheard.
7. Scheme of mind now lost a long time,
8. What is it that startles a young deer?

秦王飲酒　　李賀

極碧聲平星根笙行明更狩清艇輕泓

八目瓏今酒根吹倒殿一嬌淺年煙淡

虎空日畫酒琶腳月櫛事鳳文舞樹蠟渡眼

騎照敲飛灎琵雨喝櫛掌玉紅跌燭醉

王光知灰頭欄庭酣雲門樓絍鵁人琴

秦劍羲刻龍金洞酒銀宮花海黃仙清

KING CH'IN DRINKS WINE   *Li Ho (791–817)*

1. King Ch'in rides a tiger to roam the Eight Poles.
2. His sword's sheen brightens the sky: heaven turns sapphire.
3. Hsi-ho[1] knocks at the sun: glass jingles.
4. Ashes of kalpas at their end: peace now rules.
5. A dragon-head[2] jets out wine, inviting wine-stars.
6. Gold *p'i-p'a* lutes play, twanging deep into night.
7. Rains of Tung-t'ing Lake drum in, blowing the *sheng* pipes.
8. Drunk, he orders the moon to course backward.
9. Silver clouds, flights and rows, make jade halls glow.
10. The Gatekeeper of the palace cries out the first watch.
11. On the ornate tower, a phoenix sings a softening song.[3]
12. Silk, sea-born,[4] of scarlet patterns, flutters a clear scent.
13. Girls in yellow dance, toasting him blessings of a thousand years.
14. Candle-trees held by immortals reel out light smoke.
15. Clear lutes,[5] drunken eyes flood pools of tears.

[1] Hsi-ho, sun rider.
[2] I.e., dragon-head spout.
[3] A phoenix sings, literally, a jade phoenix's sound, refers to the resemblance of the music of the *sheng* pipes.
[4] Silk, sea-born: refers to silk woven by mermen under the sea.
[5] Also reads Green Lutes, referring to the girls, but I prefer clear lutes for poetic reasons.

北中寒　　李賀

紫死理水錢天喧懸
方龍文河如濛凌凌虹
三魚斷上大迷飛玉
敗合皮車上入水聲
黑冰木強草不海無
方河尺石花刀灣瀑
一黃三百霜輝爭山

COLD IN THE NORTH *(AFTER YÜEH-FU)* *Li Ho*

1. One side black sheen three side purple.
2. Ice closes the Yellow River: fish, dragons die.
3. Upon a three-foot bark, patterns break.
4. Chariots, a hundred pounds, go up the water.
5. Frost-flowers on grasses, huge like silver pieces.
6. A swing of sword cannot cut the misty sky.
7. Vying sea-water flies up into roars.
8. Soundless, the mountain fall: jade rainbows hang.

古悠悠行　　　李賀

白景歸西山
碧華上迢迢
今古何處盡
千歲隨風飄
海沙變成石
魚沫吹秦橋
空光遠流浪
銅柱從年消

ON AND ON: AN ANCIENT SONG (YÜEH-FU) *Li Ho*

1. White reflection retreats to western hills.
2. A jasper corona goes up into the distance.
3. The past, the present: where to end?
4. A thousand years gone with the winds.
5. Sands of the sea turn into stones.
6. Fish bubble, blast the bridge of Ch'in.
7. Light of the sky wanders far away.
8. Bronze pillars erode with the years.

巫山高　李賀

碧叢叢，高掣天。
大江翻瀾神曳煙。
楚魂尋夢風颸然。
曉風飛雨生苔錢。
瑤姬一去一千年。
丁香筇竹啼老猿。
古祠近月蟾桂寒。
椒花墜紅溼雲間。

HIGH THE MOUNT OF WU *Li Ho*

1. Emerald in big clusters
2. Pierces high sky.
3. Big river turns and tumbles, goddess pulling mist along.
4. King Ch'u's soul seeking his dream, winds sough.*
5. Morning winds, flying rains: coins of moss grow.
6. His Jade Beauty is gone, gone for a thousand years.
7. Among lilacs and bamboos, old monkeys cry.
8. Ancient shrine reaches the moon, cold amidst toads and cassis.
9. Pepper-flowers, petal by petal, drop, wet between clouds.

*King Ch'u once spent a night with Jade Beauty, goddess residing on Mount Wu, without knowing who she was. She said to the King, "In the morning, I am clouds. In the evening, I am rains."

TZ'U (LYRICS WRITTEN

TO SET TONE PATTERNS)

Both *Tz'u* (of the Sung Dynasty, 960–1279) and *Ch'ü* (of the Yüan Dynasty, 1280–1368) can briefly be defined as song-lyrics of long and short lines written according to fixed rhyme and tone patterns, the names of which were originally designations of musical airs. There are some marked stylistic differences between the two. The most obvious is, of course, the different sets of tone-patterns in operation as a result of two different musical conventions. Then, there are also the degrees of sophistication and levels of diction which can be explained partly by their origins.

Tz'u was probably born of an expansion of the *lü-shih* and *chüeh-chü* by professional singers to fit into imported musical tunes: the expansion consisting of inserting meaningless words or sounds (melisma) or repeating certain words in the line very much the way Dowland's songs were sung. When these elements were replaced by actual words, the long-and-short song-lyrics came into existence (see Glen Baxter's "Metrical Origins of the Tz'u" in Bibliography).

Ch'ü was in part connected with street operas of the common folk. In its early stage before the poets took over the form for artistic manipulation, many of these song-lyrics were replete with rustic humor and vulgar diction such as the last lines (in perfect rhymes, which I am not about to reproduce here) in a play by Tu Jen-chieh wherein a country boy expressed the woe of having to hold his "bag of urine about to explode" in order to watch more of the stage action, when the clown became so funny that he had to burst into laughter. Traces of this rustic flavor can be found even in the artistic *ch'ü* lyrics by poets. Few of the early *tz'u* lyrics contain such robustness. On the contrary and in general, they are more serious and more elaborate in diction.

Wayne Schlepp in his *San-Ch'ü* (p. 6) advanced the argument that *ch'ü* did not necessarily evolve from *tz'u*. A quick survey of some early Yüan and pre-Yüan dramas in which single pieces (*hsiao-ling*) and sets of long-lyrics (*t'ao-shu*—which were later called *ch'ü* or *san-ch'ü*) were embryonic of this form would reveal that many lines of the *tz'u* poets (such as Liu Yung) had been incorporated into a different tone pattern. Compare Liu Yung's "Bells in the Rains" to a segment of the "Recital of the Western Chamber" of Tung Chieh-yüan of the Chin Dynasty (1115-1234):

Liu:

> Cold-day cicada's cutting creak.
> Late evening before the tall pavilion.
> Sudden rains freshly still.
> Farewell drinking outside the city: no good mood.
> While hankering after all this,
> The magnolia boat is pressed to go.
> Hold hands, face to face, eyes in tears.
> Speechless, words blocked and locked.
> This departure:
> A thousand miles of smoke-waves.
> Mist in dusk sinks, sinks: Southland sky widens:
>
> All ancient men of emotion grieved over separation.
> Now this cold, deserted, clear autumn!
> Today: sober from wine? how and where?
> Willowed banks, morning winds, leftover moon.
> This departure: many years.
> Good time, great scenes, all there in vain.
> A thousand styles of sentiment I may have
> To whom can I spell them?

Tung:

> Rain suddenly stills.
> Toward evening, winds like biting.
> Hear in the withered willows cicada's cutting creak
> Not knowing after this departure
> When to meet again?
> Upon the sleeves, soaked with tears, never to end.
> Dark sorrows upon brows' peak congeal.
> How difficult to part!
> A thousand styles of sentiment I may have
> Where can I spell them?

Aspects of this musical indebtedness (the originals of the passages in question make this more obvious) are scattered throughout many of the *ch'ü* lyrics.

Both *tz'u* and *ch'ü* were originally dependent upon music and as such they share a number of similarities. It goes without saying that not all the poems can be put to music. Listening to a song and reading a poem are two quite different experiences. There is no place for intricate thought in a song: the audience would be carried along with the music and would have no time to stop and reflect as they can do in reading a poem. A poem to be set to music gives only a very simple, and even trite, emotional content and lets the music provide the texture of the emotion. Hence, many of the themes of song-lyrics, Western and Oriental alike, are love (unrequited, unfulfilled, longing), sorrow (separation, unaccountable, self-pitying), prayer, repentence, and so on, brimming with sentimental apostrophes. In spite of great masters like Su Tung-p'o who tried to inject heroic themes into the *tz'u* form and Chang Yang-hao who turned toward social problems in the *ch'ü* form, sighs of elegant sickness and refined sadness prevail in these song-lyrics. When Su introduced complex images into the *tz'u* form, he succeeded in lifting it out of the restrictions imposed by music, but then its singability was probably in question. When John Donne's "Lover's Infiniteness" was set to music, half of the poem was cut: a song cannot accommodate sophisticated thought. Only when music gives way to the importance of words could sophisticated poetry be sung and even then a special way of prolonging the chanting would be required.

Other types of musical pressure upon the poem may be cited. We have already mentioned the use of melisma and repetition of lines to fill out the measure. A reverse case can be seen in the *ch'ü*, when the original three- or five-character lines within a set tone pattern could not accommodate the meaning, extra characters would be used and these would not be given musical emphasis in singing. In Elizabethan songs there is a tendency to employ monosyllabic words to match the notes and many of the unsingable words, such as the word *dark*, would be sung as *da rke*. Chinese, being monosyllabic, is immune to such trial. Yet, the prescribed tone-patterns had some unhappy impact upon the poets' choice of rhymes. We find, for instance, some of the most often used rhymes are *-ua*, *-u*, and *-an*. They were there under the pressure of music, not that of poetic content. This is particularly obvious in the *ch'ü* in which the charm of these song-lyrics relies much more on their musicality than on their sophisticated content, which is often trite. Hence, in spite of my belief that music is untranslatable, I have made special effort to rhyme my translations in the *ch'ü* section where a little cutting of the content would not alter their musical thrust. It is more difficult to rhyme my *tz'u* translations due to the more sophisticated content; alliteration has been used as an alternative to drive the music along.

菩薩蠻　　　李白

平林漠漠煙如織
寒山一帶傷心碧
暝色入高樓
有人樓上愁

玉階空佇立
宿鳥歸飛急
何處是歸程
長亭更短亭

TUNE: "BEAUTIFUL BARBARIANS" *Li Po*

1.	level	forest	spread-out-mist-like	—	smoke	like	weave	[7]
2.	cold	mountain/s	one	belt	heart-	breaking	green	[7]
3.	dusk	color	enter	tall	tower			[5]
4.	there-is	someone	tower	top; up	sad			[5]
5.	jade	step/s	empty, in vain	stand				[5]
6.	homing	bird/s	return	fly	in-haste			[5]
7.	where	—	is	return('s)	way			[5]
8.	long	pavilion	again	short	pavilion			[5]

1. Trees shading trees, mist-smoke weaves.
2. Cold mountains, a belt, of heartbreaking green.
3. Dusk enters a high tower;
4. In it someone grieves.
5. All alone upon the jade terrace;
6. Homing birds return in haste.
7. Where is the way to return?
8. Long rest, short rest, bower after bower.

菩薩蠻　　溫庭筠

小山重疊金明滅，鬢雲欲度香腮雪。
懶起畫蛾眉，弄妝梳洗遲。

照花前後鏡，花面交相映。
新帖繡羅襦，雙雙金鷓鴣。

TUNE: "BEAUTIFUL BARBARIANS"   *Wen T'ing-yün (fl. 850)*

1.	small	mountain/s	double	fold	gold	glimmer	dim	[7]
	(upon standing curtains)						
2.	hair	cloud/s	wish-to	cross	fragrant	cheek/s	snow	[7]
3.	lazy	get-up	draw	moth-	eyebrows			[5]
4.	do	makeup	comb	wash	late			[5]
5.	reflect	flower	front	rear	mirror/s			[5]
6.	flower	face	cross	mutual	shine			[5]
7.	new(ly)	iron(ed)	embroi-dered	silk	jacket			[5]
8.	pair	pair	gold	partridge/s	—			[5]

1. Small hills upon small hills: sungold sheen comes and goes.
2. Locks of hair to cross fragrant cheeks of snow.
3. She gets up late, carefully does her eye-lining,
4. And washes and combs and powders, taking her time.
5. To reflect a flower, front mirrors again rear mirrors.
6. Flower and face, each to each, shines.
7. Newly ironed, a petticoat of embroidered silk:
8. In pairs, gold partridges, going side by side.

虞美人　　李煜

春花秋月何時了
往事知多少
小樓昨夜又東風
故國不堪回首月明中
雕闌玉砌應猶在
只是朱顏改
問君能有幾多愁
恰似一江春水向東流

1.	spring	flower/s	autumn	moon	what	time		end	[7]
2.	past	event/s	know	how	many				[5]
3.	small	tower	last	night	again	east		wind	[7]
4.	old	country	cannot-bear	look-back	moon	bright		middle	[9]
5.	carved	railing/s	jade	inlay/s	should	still		exist	[7]
6.	but; only		red faces (i.e., youthful . . .)		change				[5]
7.	ask	you	can	have	how	much		sorrow	[7]
8.	just	like a	river	spring	water	toward	east	flow	[9]

1. Spring flowers, autumn moon: when to end?
2. The past: how much is known?
3. Upon the tower last night, east winds blow again.
4. Native country: unbearable to look back amidst the bright moon.
5. Carved railings, jade inlays should still be there,
6. Only faces are changed.
7. How much sorrow do you have?
8. The way a spring river eastward flows.

御街行　　　范仲海

紛紛墜葉飄香砌。夜寂靜，寒聲碎。真珠簾捲玉樓空，天淡銀河垂地。年年今夜，月華如練，長是人千里。

愁腸已斷無由醉。酒未到，先成淚。殘燈明滅枕頭欹，諳盡孤眠滋味。都來此事，眉間心上，無計相迴避。

TUNE: "WALK ON THE IMPERIAL STREET"

Fan Chung-yen (989–1052)

1. Confused leaves fall, fluttering fragrant steps.
2. Night stills.
3. Cold cracks.
4. Bead-blinds rolled up: jade chamber is empty.
5. Sky thins: Milky Way touches the ground.
6. This night each year
7. Moonlight shines like silk.
8. Always the loved one a thousand miles away!
9. Guts cut by grief, no way to get drunk.
10. Before wine gets there
11. Tears form.
12. Dying lamp flickers, pillow aslant,
13. Darkens the taste of solitary bed.
14. This matter as always
15. Between brows, in the heart,
16. No trick to escape.

雨霖鈴　　　柳永

寒蟬淒切，晚歇飲無緒。對長亭初帳處，都門戀舟催發。留戀蘭舟催發，執手相看淚眼，竟無語凝噎。念去去千里煙波，暮靄沈沈楚天闊。

多情自古傷離別，更那堪冷落清秋節。今宵酒醒何處，楊柳岸曉風殘月。此去經年，應是良辰好景虛設。便縱有千種風情，更與何人說。

TUNE: "BELLS IN THE RAINS" *Liu Yung (fl. 1045)*

1. Cold-day cicada's cutting creak.
2. Late evening before the tall pavilion.
3. Sudden rains freshly still.
4. Farewell drinking outside the city: no good mood.
5. While hankering after all this,
6. The magnolia boat is pressed to go.
7. Hold hands, face to face, eyes in tears.
8. Speechless, words blocked and locked.
9. This departure:
10. A thousand miles of smoke-waves.
11. Mist in dusk sinks, sinks: Southland sky widens.

12. All ancient men of emotion grieved over separation.
13. Now this cold, deserted, clear autumn!
14. Today: sober from wine? how and where?
15. Willowed banks, morning winds, leftover moon.
16. This departure: many years.
17. Good times, great scenes, all there in vain.
18. A thousand styles of sentiment I may have
19. To whom can I spell them?

念奴嬌　赤壁懷古　　　　　　蘇東坡

大江東去，浪淘盡，千古風流人物。故壘西邊，人道是，三國周郎赤壁。亂石崩雲，驚濤裂岸，捲起千堆雪。江山如畫，一時多少豪傑。

遙想公瑾當年，小喬初嫁了，雄姿英發。羽扇綸巾，談笑間，強虜灰飛煙滅。故國神遊，多情應笑我，早生華髮。人生如夢，一尊還酹江月。

318

TUNE: "CHARMING NIEN-NU" *Su Tung-p'o (1036–1101)*

1. Eastward goes the Yangtze!
2. Waves scour all
3. Free-soaring worthies of all years.
4. West of the ancient fortress,
5. They say:
6. Three Kingdoms, Master Chou, Red Cliffs,*
7. Thrown-out rocks breaking clouds.
8. Startling surges tear at banks,
9. Roll up a thousand heaps of snow.
10. Mountains, rivers—all picture!
11. One historic moment: how many heroes!
12. Think of Kung-chin back in those years—
13. Little Ch'iao newly married—†
14. Heroic gait in full swing:
15. Feathered fan, silk scarf.
16. Between talks and laughs,
17. The chief enemy ashens in winds, gone in smoke.
18. Spiritual tour of the ancient kingdom . . .
19. Sentimental! yes, flout at me
20. At my early white hair.
21. Life is dream!
22. A bottle to offer to the river-moon.

*During the Three Kingdoms (Wei, Shu, Wu), Master Chou, alias
Kung-chin, chief military adviser of the Wu forces, won a decisive victory
from Ts'ao Ts'ao of Wei by burning his fleet at Red Cliffs.
†Little Ch'iao is the younger daughter of Ch'iao Hsuan of Eastern Han
married to Chou.

臨江仙　　蘇東坡

醉後更雷鳴

醒後三已應聲
坡歸鼻息都不江
東琴鼻都聽
飲來童門
夜歸家敲倚杖

有平
我營紋平
非營縠逝
身却靜此逝
此忘風從餘生
恨時闌舟寄餘
長何夜小江海寄

TUNE: "IMMORTAL BY THE RIVER" *Su Tung-p'o*

1. night	drink	East	Slope	wake	again	drunk	[7]
2. return	—	it-seems	third	watch			[6]
3. home	boy	nose-breath	already	thundering	—		[7]
4. knock	door	all	no	response			[5]
5. lean	staff	listen	river	sound			[5]
6. long	regret	this	body	not	my	possession	[7]
7. when	—	forget	—	busy-buzz			[6]
8. night	deep	wind	quiet	waves	—	smooth	[7]
9. small	boat	from	here	gone drift			[5]
10. river	sea	entrust	rest-	of-life			[5]

1. Drinking into deep night at East Slope, sober then drunk.
2. I return home perhaps at small hours,
3. My page-boy's snoring already like thunder.
4. No answer to my knocking at the door,
5. I lean on my staff to listen to the river rushing.
6. I grieve forever that this body, no body of mine.
7. When can I forget this buzzing life?
8. Night now still, wind quiet, waves calm and smooth,
9. A little boat to drift from here.
10. On the river, on the sea, my remaining years.

清平樂　　黃庭堅

春歸何處
寂寞無行路
若有人知春去處
喚取歸來同住

春無蹤跡誰知
除非問取黃鸝
百囀無人能解
因風飛過薔薇

TUNE: "CH'ING-P'ING SONG" *Huang T'ing-chien (1045–1105)*

1. spring	return	where	—				[4]
2. loneliness	—	no	walk	road			[5]
3. if	there-is	someone	know	spring('s)	whereabouts	—	[7]
4. call	—	return	—	live	together		[6]
5. spring	no	trace	—	who	know		[6]
6. except	—	ask	—	yellow	oriole/s		[6]
7. hundred	tune/s	no	one	can	understand		[6]
8. because-of	wind	fly	past	roses	—		[6]

1. Where does Spring return?
2. All solitary: no road.
3. If someone knows where Spring goes,
4. Call Spring back to stay.

5. Spring leaves no trace. Who knows?
6. But to ask the yellow orioles.
7. A hundred songs: no one understands—
8. With the winds, fly over the roses.

蘭陵王　周邦彥

柳陰直
煙裡絲絲弄碧
隋隄上
曾見幾番
拂水飄綿送行色？
登臨望故國
誰識
京華倦客？
長亭路
年去歲來
應折柔條過千尺

閑尋舊蹤跡
又酒趁哀絃
燈照離席
梨花榆火催寒食
愁一箭風快
半篙波暖
回頭迢遞便數驛
望人在天北

324

TUNE: "PRINCE LAN-LING" *Chou Pang-yen (1057–1121)*

1. Willows shadows hang straight
2. In the smoke, lines of silk, in green sheen,
3. Upon the dam
4. How many times
5. Fluttering water, floating catkins, sending off friends?
6. I ascend to view my home country.
7. Who knows
8. This tired traveler of the Capital?
9. Tall Pavilion Road:
10. Years come years go,
11. They must have broken off soft branches a thousand feet!
12. I sometimes look for old footprints.
13. Again wine to whining strings.
14. Lamps brightening farewell tables.
15. Pear blossoms, flaming elms quicken the Cold Food Day.
16. Sorrow, one shaft, faster than wind.
17. Punting halfway of warming waves,
18. I look back into the distance to count the mail-posts,
19. Longing for friends at sky's north end.

悽惻。
恨堆積。
漸別浦縈廻，
津堠岑寂。
斜陽冉冉春無極。
念月榭攜手，
露橋聞笛。
沈思前事，
似夢裡，
淚暗滴。

20. Stricken
21. Grief teeming up.
22. Separation: water twists and turns.
23. Garrisoned fords all quiet.
24. Sun slants slowly: spring, no end.
25. Under the moon, hand in hand.
26. Dew-dappled bridge: to listen to flutes.
27. Think of things past:
28. Like dream,
29. Tears darkly drip.

如夢令　　李清照

昨夜雨疏風驟
濃睡不消殘酒
試問捲簾人依舊
却道海棠
知否
知否
應是綠肥紅瘦

TUNE: "DREAM SONG"　*Li Ch'ing-chao (1081–?)*

1. last	night	rain	sparse	wind	sudden	[6]
2. deep	slumber	not	dispel	remaining	wine	[6]
3. try	ask	roll-	blind-	person		[5]
4. but	say	begonia	—	remain-	the-same	[6]
5. know	?					[2]
6. know	?					[2]
7. should-be	—	green	fat	red	thin	[6]

1. Last night, scattering rains, sudden winds.
2. Deep sleep abates not the remaining wine.
3. Try ask he who rolls up the blind:
4. Thinking the begonia blooming as before.
5. Know it?
6. Know it?
7. Fattening leaves' green, thinning petals' red.

釵頭鳳　　陸游

紅酥手，黃縢酒，滿城春色宮牆柳。東風惡，歡情薄，一懷愁緒，幾年離索。錯！錯！錯！

春如舊，人空瘦，淚痕紅浥鮫綃透。桃花落，閑池閣，山盟雖在，錦書難托。莫！莫！莫！

TUNE: "HAIRPIN PHOENIX" *Lu Yu (1125–1209)*

1. Rouged hands.
2. Yellow wine.
3. A city of spring, walls of willows.
4. The east wind is wicked,
5. Togetherness now dispersed.
6. A bosom of confused silk.
7. Many years of separation.
8. Wrong! Wrong! Wrong!
9. Spring as before.
10. You, thin for no end.
11. Tears streak pink soaking shagreen silk.
12. Peach blossoms fall.
13. Bower of Leisure Pond.
14. Vows are there;
15. A letter, no way to send:
16. No! No! No!

辛棄疾

西江月

醉裡且貪歡笑，要愁那得工夫。近來始覺古人書，信著全無是處。

昨夜松邊醉倒，問松我醉何如。只疑松動要來扶，以手推松曰去。

330

TUNE: "MOON OF THE WESTERN RIVER"

Hsin Ch'i-chi (1140–1207)

1.	drunk (in drunkenness)	within	but	seek	happy (merriment)	laughter		[6]
2.	wish-to	be-sad	where-to-	—	get-time			[6]
3.	recently	—	then	under-stand	ancient	men('s)	book/s	[7]
4.	believe	(them)	all	no	good	point		[6]
5.	last	night	pine	side	drunk	fall		[6]
6.	ask	pine	I	drunk	how-is-it			[6]
7.	only	suspect	pine	move	wish-to	come	hold (me)	[7]
8.	use	hand	push	pine	say	go		[6]

1. While drunk, I seek merriment.
2. To get sad—where is the time?
3. Recently, about ancient books I feel
4. To believe them—none is of any use.

5. Last night I got drunk beside a pine.
6. I asked it: how is my drunken way?
7. Suspecting the pine would rise to hold me up,
8. I pushed it and said: Go!

CH'Ü (SONGS, ORIGINATED FROM YÜAN DRAMA,

THE SET TONE-PATTERNS OF WHICH

WERE SUBSEQUENTLY ADOPTED

TO FORM A NEW GENRE)

大德歌　關漢卿

風飄飄

雨瀟瀟

便做陳摶也睡不著

懊惱傷懷抱

撲簌簌淚點抛

秋蟬兒噪罷寒蛩兒叫

淅零零細雨打芭蕉

TUNE: "VAST VIRTUE" *Kuan Han-ch'ing*

(ca. 1220–ca. 1300)

1.	wind/s	manner-of-blowing								[3]
2.	rain/s	manner-of-raining								[3]
3.	(even)*	Chen	Po	(also)	sleep	not	—			[5]
	(to be)	(famous for sleeping for days on end)								
4.	grief	—	hurt	bosom	—					[5]
5.	rustling	—	tear	drop/s	throw					[5]
6.	autumn	cicada/s	(—)	make-noise	end	cold	cricket/s	(—)	cry	[7]
7.	manner-of-dripping	(small)	rain/s	beat	banana					[6]

1. Winds whistle.
2. Rains drizzle.
3. Even the Sleep Immortal cannot go to sleep.
4. Sorrow meshed on heart's tip.
5. Downpour, downpour, tears drop.
6. Chilling cicadas stop, crickets creak.
7. Drip, drip, fine rains on banana-leaves beat.

*Small characters in the Chinese original and hence annotations within parentheses are extra characters added to the original *pattern* to fill out the meaning. For instance, although there are 8 characters in this line, only 5 are sung to music, presumably. Or perhaps we shuold say only 5 are given musical emphasis. Such practice is very common in Ch'ü and is not counted as out of pattern.

四塊玉　關漢卿

舊酒沒
新醅潑
老瓦盆邊笑呵呵
共山僧野叟閒吟和
他出一對雞
我出一個鵝
閒快活

TUNE: "FOUR PIECES OF JADE"   *Kuan Han-ch'ing*

1.	old	wine	no-more				[3]
2.	new	brew	pour; brim				[3]
3.	old	earthenware	—	side	laugh	"ho-ho"	[7]
4.	(with)	mountain	monk	rustic	old man	at-leisure	chant- [7]
							harmonize
5.	he	offer	(a pair of)	chicken/s			[3]
6.	I	offer	(a)	goose			[3]
7.	at-leisure	make	merry				[3]

1. Old wine gone.
2. New brew is on.
3. Beside an old jug, laugh our heads off.
4. Mountain monk, rustic old man, in turn we chant.
5. He offers a pair of chickens.
6. I offer a goose—
7. And let ourselves all loose.

沈醉東風　　盧摯

恰離了綠水青山那搭
早來到竹籬茅舍人家
野花路畔開
村酒槽頭榨
真吃的欠欠答答
醉了山童不勤咱
白頭上亂插黃花

TUNE: "DRUNK IN THE EAST WIND" *Lu Chih (1234–1300)*

1. (just left)
   green   water   greenish -blue   mountain   that   place   [6]

2. (early arrive)
   bamboo   fence   straw   house/s   people's   home/s   [6]

3. (wild flowers)
   road   side   bloom   [3]

4. (village wine)
   wine-press   squeeze   [3]

5. straight   drink   drunken-manner-somewhat-dazed   [7]

6. drunk   —   mountain   boy   not   advise   us   [7]

7. white   head/s   above   undiscri-minately   plant   yellow   flower/s   [7]

---

1. (Soon after)
   The blue-water, green-mountain shore,

2. (We came to)
   Bamboo-fenced homes of straw.

3. (Wild flowers)
   Blooming by the road.

4. (Village wine)
   To the wine-press.

5. Drink to a dead dull daze.

6. Flustered, mountain boys leave all advice behind.

7. Upon our white heads, plant yellow flowers, any kind.

天 淨 沙　　馬致遠

枯籐老樹昏鴉
小橋流水人家
古道西風瘦馬
夕陽西下
斷腸人在天涯

TUNE: "SKY-PURE SAND"　*Ma Chih-yüan (ca. 1260–ca. 1324)*

1.	withered	vine/s	old	tree/s	evening	crow/s	[6]
2.	small	bridge	flowing	water	man's	house/s	[6]
3.	ancient	road	west	wind	lean	horse	[6]
4.	evening	sun	west	down			[4]
5.	broken	gut	man	at	sky	edge	[6]
	(broken-hearted)						

1. Dried vines, an old tree, evening crows;
2. A small bridge, flowing water, men's homes;
3. An ancient road, west winds, a lean horse;
4. Sun slants west:
5. The heart-torn man at sky's end.

落梅風　馬致遠

夕陽下
酒斿閑
兩三航未曾著岸
落花水香茅舍晚
斷橋頭賣魚人散

TUNE: "WINDS OF FALLING PLUMS" *Ma Chih-yüan*

1.	sun	set	below					[3]
2.	wine	flag	at-leisure					[3]
3.	two	three	boat/s	not	yet	reach	bank	[7]
4.	falling	flower/s	water	fragrant	straw	home/s	late	[7]
5.	broken	bridge	head	sell-	fish-	men	scatter	[7]

1. Under the afterglow,
2. Wine-flags are slow.
3. Yet to reach the shore—two three boats.
4. Falling flowers, scented water, straw huts in the dusk.
5. At a broken bridgehead: scattering fishmongers homeward go.

清江引　馬致遠

樵夫覺来山月低
釣叟来尋覓
你把柴斧抛
我把魚船棄
尋取但穩便處閒坐

TUNE: "SONG OF CLEAR RIVER"   *Ma Chih-yüan*

1.	woodcutter	—	wake	—	mountain	moon	low	[7]
2.	fishing	old man	come	seek; visit	—			[5]
3.	you	—	firewood/s	ax	throw			[5]
4.	I	—	fishing	boat	discard	leisurely		[5]
5.	seek-out	—	(a) stable	convenient-(place)			sit	[7]

1. Woodcutter wakes up: mountain moon is low.
2. Fisherman comes to visit.
3. You throw away firewoods and ax,
4. I throw away my fishing boat,
5. To find a neat little corner to sit and relax.

滿庭芳　　姚燧

浦沙湖頭聚，煮沽，旋須，烟月，荻蘆。釣淺平畫灘呼和，相剌多帶月物野葫蘆。收籠滿，来語有無中青盡。帆烟水晚，笑魚酒盤山且。

TUNE: "FULL COURT OF FRAGRANCE"   *Yao Sui (1239–1314)*

1.	sail	rolled-up	fishing	shore				[4]
2.	smoke	shroud	shallow	sand				[4]
3.	water	full	flat; smooth (name)	lake				[4]
4.	dusk	time	all	beach	head	gather		[6]
5.	laugh	talk	mutual	call				[4]
6.	fish	there-is	remaining	with	smoke	twirl	cook	[7]
7.	wine	not	much	carry	moon	must	buy	[7]
8.	tray (i.e., dishes)	inside	thing/s					[3]
9.	mountain	food	wild	vegetable/s				[4]
10.	let's	end; empty	gourd-bottle/s					[4]

1. Furl sails into fishermen's cove.
2. Smoke shrouds the shallow sand.
3. Water brims the Smooth Lake.
4. Evening comes: every step shoreward bend,
5. Laughing, talking, calling each other.
6. Leftover fish: cook in a smoke-swirling pan.
7. Not enough wine: go buy, through miles of moonlight.
8. For food now:
9. Mountain dishes, wild vegetables.
10. Let's empty all the gourd-bottles.

山坡羊　　張養浩

峰巒如聚，波濤如怒，山河表裏潼關路。望西都，意躊躇。傷心秦漢經行處，宮闕萬間都做了土。興，百姓苦；亡，百姓苦。

1. peak/s	—	like	gather				[4]
2. wave/s	—	like	angry				[4]
3. mountain	river	outside	inside	T'ung	Pass	road	[7]
4. look	west	capital					[3]
5. thought/s	hesitate						[3]
6. broken-hearted	—	Ch'in Dynasties	Han	passing place (i.e., where they, the armies of Ch'in and Han, passed)	—		[7]
7. palaces	—	ten-thousand	—	make	—	earth	[7]
8. rise							[1]
9. commonfolks	suffer						[3]
10. fall							[1]
11. commonfolks	suffer						[3]

1. Peaks gather.
2. Waves in anger.
3. Between mountains and rivers, the T'ung Pass coils.
4. Looking toward the West Capital—
5. My thoughts all in turmoil.
6. Where the Ch'in and Han armies passed, my heart is sorrow-filled.
7. A million palaces built and rebuilt.
8. Kingdoms rise,
9. The commonfolks suffer.
10. Kingdoms fall,
11. The commonfolks suffer.

山坡羊　　劉致

朝朝瓊樹

家家朱戶

驕嘶過沽酒樓前路

貴何如

賤何如

六橋都是經行處

花落水流深院宇

閒

天定許

忙

人自取

TUNE: "SHEEP ON THE MOUNTAIN SLOPE" *Liu Chih (14th century)*

1.	morning	morning	jade	tree				[4]
2.	house	house	red	mansion				[4]
3.	(proudly)	neighing	past	sell-wine-house	front	road		[7]
4.	high-position	how						[3]
5.	low-position	how						[3]
6.	six of the West Lake	bridge/s	all	are	passing (i.e., where we pass)	place		[7]
7.	flower/s	fall	water	flow	deep	court	hall	[7]
8.	leisure							[1]
9.	sky	ordain	allow					[3]
10.	busyness							[1]
11.	man	self	take					[3]

1. Every morning, emerald trees.
2. Every house, made of ruby.
3. Horses neigh on the road before the tavern.
4. High position: what is it?
5. Low position: what is it?
6. All six bridges we have crossed.
7. Flowers fall, water flows in deep courts and halls.
8. Leisure is
9. Heaven-given.
10. Busyness is
11. All manmade.

撥不斷　　　張可久

墓田鵶
故宮花
慜烟恨　水　丹　青　畫
峻宇雕　牆　宰　相　家
夕陽芳　草　漁　樵　話
百年之　下

TUNE: "UNBROKEN"　*Chang K'o-chiu (ca. 1280–ca. 1330)*

1.	tomb	field	crow/s					[3]
2.	old	palace	flower/s					[3]
3.	sad	smoke	sorrowful	water	Chinese-	paints	picture	[7]
4.	tall	house	carved	wall	premier	—	house	[7]
5.	sun	set	fragrant	flower	fisherman	woodcutters	talk	[7]
6.	hundred	years	below					[4]
	(since . . .)							

1. Graveyard crows.
2. Old palace flowers.
3. Smoke and water and ink-paintings filled with sorrows.
4. High halls, carved walls, premier's bowers.
5. Sunset, scented grasses, fishermen and woodcutters' hours.
6. A hundred years, O!

迎 仙 客　　　張可久

雲 冉 冉
草 纖 纖
誰 家 隱 居 山 半 崦
水 烟 寒
溪 路 險
半 幅 青 簾
五 里 桃 花 店

TUNE: "TRAVELER WELCOMING THE IMMORTAL"

Chang K'o-chiu

1.	cloud/s	slow-moving	—					[3]
2.	grass	slender	slender					[3]
3.	whose	house	hidden	live	mountain	half	hill	[7]
4.	water	smoke	cold					[3]
5.	stream	path	difficult					[3]
6.	half	green	curtain					[4]
7.	five	mile	peach	blossom	inn			[5]

1. Clouds seen and unseen.
2. Grass thin and green.
3. Whose house hidden half up the hill?
4. Smoke-water's chill.
5. Path along the stream full of peril.
6. Half a curtain green.
7. Five-mile Peach Petal Inn.

351

殿前歡　　張可久

望長安
前程渺渺鬢斑斑
南來北往隨征雁
行路艱難
青泥小劍閣岸
紅葉溢江雲棧
白草連半紙
功名雪千山

TUNE: "MERRIMENT BEFORE THE PALACE HALL"

Chang K'o-chiu

1. looking-toward	Ch'ang-	an					[3]
2. front (i.e., future)	route	misty-unclear	temple-hair	white	white		[7]
3. south	come	north	go	follow	traveling	geese	[7]
4. travel-on-the-road	difficult	—					[4]
5. green mud	little	sword	pass				[5]
6. red leaf	Pen	river	bank				[3]
7. white	grass	connect	cloud	plank-path			[5]
8. rank	name	half	paper				[4]
9. wind	snow	thousand	mountain/s				[4]

1. Toward Ch'ang-an—
2. Future course, all blurred; sideburns now white.
3. Go south go north following migrant geese's flight.
4. Traveling is a plight.
5. Up Green Mud Sword Pass.
6. Down Red Leaf River Pen.
7. White grass reaches the sky.
8. Name and rank: only half a sheet of paper.
9. Windblown snow, a thousand mountains, flies.

SELECTED BIBLIOGRAPHY

BIBLIOGRAPHIES

Bibliography of Asian Studies. 1956–.

Davidson, Martha. *A list of Published Translations from Chinese to English, French and German.* Part II. Poetry. New Haven, Conn., 1957.

Gordon, H. D., and Shulman, Frank. *Doctoral Dissertations on China. A Bibliography of Studies in Western Languages, 1945–1970.* Seattle, 1972.

Hucker, Charles O. *China: A Critical Bibliography.* Tucson, Ariz., 1962.

Lust, John. *Index Sinicus: A Catalogue of Articles Relating to China in Periodicals and other Collective Publications 1920–1955.* Cambridge, 1964.

Stucki, Curtis W. *American Doctoral Dissertations on Asia, 1933–1958.* Ithaca, N.Y., 1959.

Yuan, Tung-li. *China in Western Literature.* New Haven, Conn., 1958.

INTRODUCTORY WORKS AND RELATED SPECIAL STUDIES

Birch, Cyril, ed. *Studies in Chinese Literary Genres.* Berkeley, Los Angeles, London, 1974.

——. "The Language of Chinese Literature," *New Literary History,* IV.1 (1972), 141–150.

Chow, Tse-tsung. "The Early History of the Chinese Word *Shih* (Poetry)." In *Wen-lin,* Ed. Chow Tse-tsung. Madison, Wis., 1968.

Hightower, James Robert. *Topics in Chinese Literature.* Rev. ed. Cambridge, Mass., 1965.

Liu, James J. Y. *The Art of Chinese Poetry.* Chicago, 1962.

Liu, Wu-chi. *An Introduction to Chinese Literature.* Bloomington, Ind. and London, 1966.

Watson, Burton. *Chinese Lyricism.* New York, 1971.

Yip, Wai-lim. "The Chinese Poem: Some Aspects of the Problem of Syntax in Translation." In *Ezra Pound's Cathay.* Princeton, 1969.

THE BOOK OF SONGS

Chen, Shih-hsiang. "The Shih-ching: Its Generic Significance in Chinese Literary History and Poetics," *Bulletin of the Institute of History and Philology, Academia Sinica,* Vol. XXXIX, pt. 1 (1969), 371–413.

Dobson, W. A. C. H. *The Language of the Book of Songs.* Toronto, 1968.

Granet, Marcel. *Festivals and Songs of Ancient China*. London, 1932.

Hsu, Vivian C. W. Ling. "The Political Usage of Song in Ancient China," *Tamkang Review*, I.2 (1970), 201–226.

Kennedy, George A. "Metrical Irregularity in the *Shih Ching*," *Harvard Journal of Asiatic Studies*, 4 (1939), 284–296.

———. "A Note on Ode 220." In *G. A. Kennedy's Selected Works*. Ed. Tien-yi Li, New Haven, Conn., 1964.

Legge, James. "Prolegomena" to Vol. 4 of *The Chinese Classics*. Hong Kong reprint, 1961.

McNaughton, William. *The Book of Songs*. New York, 1971.

Mekada, Makato. "On 'Hsing'—a Technique of Expression in the Poetry of Ancient China," *Bulletin of the Faculty of Literature*, Kyushu University, 2 (1954), 31–42.

Wang, C. H. *The Bell and the Drum; A Study of Shih Ching as Formulaic Poetry*. Berkeley, Los Angeles, London, 1974.

Watson, Burton. *Early Chinese Literature*. New York, 1962. Also touches upon *Shih Ching*.

CH'U TZ'U

Chen, Shih-hsiang. "The Genesis of Poetic Time: The Greatness of Ch'ü Yüan, with a New Critical Approach," *Tsing Hua Journal of Chinese Studies*, X.1 (1973), 1–44.

Graham, A. C. "The Prosody of the Sao Poem in the Ch'u Tz'u," *Asia Major*, X.2 (1963), 119–161.

Hawkes, David. "Introduction" to *Ch'u Tz'u*. Oxford, 1959.

———. "The Quest of the Goddess," *Asia Major*, XIII (1967), 71–94.

Hightower, James Robert. "Ch'ü Yüan Studies" in *Silver Jubilee Volume of the Zinbun-Kagaken-Kenkyusho*, Kyoto University, Kyoto, 1954. Pp. 192–223.

Waley, Arthur. *The Nine Songs: A Study of Shamanism in Ancient China*. London, 1955.

Wang, C. H. "Sartorial Emblems and the Quest: A Comparative Study of the *Li Sao* and the *Faerie Queene*," *Tamkang Review*, II.2 & III.1 (1971/1972), 309–328.

LANDSCAPE POETRY

Eoyang, Eugene. "The Solitary Boat: Images of Self in Chinese Nature Poetry," *Journal of Asian Studies*, XXXII.4 (1973), 593–621.

Frankel, Hans H. "The 'I' in Chinese Lyric Poetry," *Oriens*, 10 (1951), 128–136.

Frodsham, J. D. 'The Origins of Chinese Nature Poetry, *Asia Major*, VIII (1960), 68–104.

———. "The Nature Poetry of Pao Chao," *Orient/West*, VIII.6 (1963), 85–93.

———. "The Poet Juan Chi," *Journal of the Chinese Society, Malaya University*, 2 (1963/1964), 26–42.

———. *The Murmuring Stream*. 2 vols. Kuala Lumpur, 1967.

———. "Landscape Poetry in China and Europe," *Comparative Literature*, XIX.3 (1967), 193–215.

Hightower, James Robert. *The Poetry of T'ao Ch'ien*. New York, 1967.

Kuo, Ta-hsia. *Pao Chao*. New York, forthcoming.

Li, Chi. "The Changing Concept of the Recluse in Chinese Literature," *Harvard Journal of Asiatic Studies*, 24 (1963), 234–247.

Mather, Richard. "The Landscape Buddhism of the Fifth Century Poet Hsieh Ling-yün," *Journal of Asian Studies*, XVII.1 (1958), 67–79.

———. "The Mystical Ascent of the T'ien T'ai Mountains: Sun Cho's Yu-t'ien-t'ai-shan Fu," *Monumenta Serica*, XX (1961), 226–245.

Mei, Y. P. "Man and Nature in Chinese Literature," in *Proceedings*, Indiana Conference on Oriental-Western Literary Relations, ed. H. Frenz and G. L. Anderson. Chapel Hill, N.C., 1955. Pp. 163–173.

Miller, James While. "English Romanticism and Chinese Nature Poetry," *Comparative Literature*, XXIV. 2 (1972), 216–236.

Tung, Constantine. "Juan Chi, an Escapist, and His Inescapable World," *Journal of the Blaisdell Institute*, V.2 (1970), 9–22.

YÜEH-FU

Frankel, Hans A. "The Formulaic Language of the Chinese Ballad 'South-east Flies the Peacocks,' *Bulletin of the Institute of History and Philology, Academia Sinica* XXIV.2 (1969), 219–244.

Ogawa, Tamaki. "The Song of Ch'ih-lê," *Acta Asiatica*, 1 (1960), 43–56.

Roy, David T. "The Theme of the Neglected Wife in the Poetry of Ts'ao Chih," *Journal of Asian Studies*, XIX. 1 (1959), 25–31.

Schindler, B. "The Dramatic Character of the Old Chinese Harvest Songs," *Gaster Memoriae* (1936), pp. 498–502.

Wang, Yün-hsi. "The Yüeh-fu Songs of Ancient China," *Chinese Literature*, 4 (1959), 110–117.

Wivell, Charles J. "The Chinese Oral and Pseudo-Oral Narrative Traditions," *Transactions*, International Conference of Orientalists in Japan, 16 (1971), 53–65.

Yu, Kuan-ying. "The Yüeh-fu Folk Songs of the Han Dynasty," *Chinese Literature*, 5 (1963), 67–74.

CHÜEH-CHÜ AND LÜ-SHIH (T'ANG POETRY)

Altieri, Daniel P. "The Kan-Yü of Chang Chiu-ling: Poems of Political Tragedy," *Tamkang Review*, IV.1 (1973), 63–73.

Bishop, John L. "Prosodic Elements in T'ang Poetry," in *Proceedings*, Indiana Conference on Oriental-Western Literary Relations, ed. H. Frenz and G. L. Anderson. Chapel Hill, N.C., 1955. Pp. 49–63.

Chen, David Y. "Li Ho and Keats: Poverty, Illness, Frustration and a Poetic Career." *Tsing Hua Journal of Chinese Studies*, V.1 (1965), 67–84.

Chen, Shih-hsiang. "To Circumvent 'The Design of Eightfold Array'," *Tsing Hua Journal of Chinese Studies*, VII.1 (1968), 26–53.

Chi, Ch'iu-lang. "A Comparative Approach to Late T'ang Poetry," *Tamkang Review*, II.2 & III.1 (1971/1972), 269–277.

Cooper, Arthur. "Introduction" to *Li Po and Tu Fu*. Baltimore, 1973.

Davis, Albert R. *Tu Fu*. New York, 1971.

Feifel, Eugene. "Biography of Po Chü-i—Annotated translation from Chüan 166 of the Chiu T'ang Shu," *Monumenta Serica*, XVII (1958), 255–311.

Frankel, Hans H. "T'ang Literati: A Composite Biography." In *Confucian Personalities*. Ed. Arthur F. Wright and Denis Twitchett. Stanford, 1962.

——. *Biographies of Meng Hao-jan*. 3d ed. Berkeley and Los Angeles, 1966.

——. "The Contemplation of the Past in T'ang Poetry." In *ACLS Conference on T'ang Studies*. Cambridge, 1969.

Frodsham, J. D. "Introduction" to *The Poems of Li Ho*. New York, 1970.

Graham, A. C. "Introduction" to *Poems of Late T'ang*. Baltimore, 1965.

Hawkes, David. *A Little Premier of Tu Fu*. London, 1967.

Hsueh, Feng-sheng. "Elements in the Metrics of T'ang Poetry," *Bulletin of the Institute of History and Philology, Academia Sinica*, XXXXII (1972), 467–488.

Hung, William. *Tu Fu*. Cambridge, Mass., 1952.

Lattimore, David. "Textual Allusion and T'ang Poetry." In *ACLS Conference on T'ang Studies*. Cambridge, 1969.

Levy, Howard. "Rainbow Skirt and Feather Jacket," *Literature East and West*, XIII.1/2 (1969), 111–140.

Liu, James J. Y. *The Poetry of Li Shang-yin*. Chicago, 1969.

Mei, Tsu-lin, and Kao, Yu-kung. "Tu Fu's 'Autumn Meditations': An Exercise in Linguistic Criticism," *Harvard Journal of Asiatic Studies*, 28 (1968), 44–80.

——. "Syntax, Diction, and Imagery in T'ang Poetry," *Harvard Journal of Asiatic Studies*, 31 (1971), 49–136.

Nielson, Thomas. *The T'ang Poet-monk Chiao-jan*. Tempe, Ariz., 1972.

——. *Wei Ying-wu*. New York, forthcoming.

Nienhauser, Jr., William H. et al. *Liu Tsung-Yüan*. New York, 1971.

Schafer, Edward H. *The Divine Women: Dragon Ladies and Rain Maidens in T'ang Literature*. Berkeley, Los Angeles, London, 1974.

South, Margaret Tudor. *Li Ho, a Scholar-Official of the Yuan-ho Period, 806–821*. Adelaide, Australia, 1967.

Stimson, Hugh M. "The Sound of a T'ang Poem: 'Grieving about Greenslope' by Duh-Fuu," *Journal of the American Oriental Society*, 89 (1969), 59–67.

Tan, Mabel. "Conformity and Originality in the Poetry of Tu Mu (803–852)," *Literature East and West*, XV.2 (1971), 244–259.

Tsukimura, Reiko. "Li Shang-yin's Poetry: Three Ways of Looking at The Inner Reality—Introspection, Recollection and Vision," *Literature East and West*, XI.3 (1967), 273–291.

Waley, Arthur. *The Life and Time of Po Chü-i*. London. 1949.

——. *The Poetry and Career of Li Po*. London, 1950.

Walmsley, Lewis C., and Walmsley, Dorothy B. *Wang Wei, the Painter-Poet*. Rutland, Vt., 1968.

Wang, Ch'iu-kuei. *'Objective Correlative' in the Love Poems of Li Shang-yin*. Taipei, 1970.

Wells, Henry G. "Tu Fu and the Aesthetics of Poetry," *Literature East and West*, XI. 3 (1967), 238–249.

Wong, Shirleen. "The Quatrain (chüeh-chü) of Tu Fu," *Monumenta Serica*, XXIX (1970/1971), 142–162.

Wu, John C. H. *The Four Seasons of T'ang Poetry*. Rutland, Vt., and Tokyo, 1972.

Yen, Yuan-shu. "Since Your Departure—An Analysis," *Tamkang Review*, III.2 (1972), 253–266.

——. "Pear Blossom in Spring Rain: A Reading of 'Chang Hen Ko,'" *Tamkang Review*, IV.1 (1973), 129–146.

Yip, Wai-lim. "One Case in the Translation of the Voice in a Poem: Exterior or Interior Dialogue?" *Delos* 4 (1970), 202–207.

——. "Wang Wei and the Aesthetics of Pure Experience." In *Hiding the Universe*. New York, 1972.

Yoshikawa, Kojiro. "Tu Fu's Poetics and Poetry." *Acta Asiatica*, 16 (1969), 1–26.

Yu, Kwang-chung. "To the White Jade Palace: A Critical Study of Li Ho (791–817)," *Tamkang Journal*, VII (1968), 193–225.

SUNG LYRICS

Baxter, Glen W. "Metrical Origins of the Tz'u," *Harvard Journal of Asiatic Studies*, 16 (1953), 108–145.

Chao, Chia-ying Yeh. "Wu Wen Ying's Tz'u: A Modern View," *Harvard Journal of Asiatic Studies*, 28 (1968), 53–92.

Chen, shih-chuan. "The Rise of the Tz'u Reconsidered," *Journal of Asian Studies*, XC.2 (1971), 232–242.

Cheng, chien. "Su Tung-p'o and Hsin Chia-hsüan: A Comparison," *Tamkang Review*, I.2 (1970), 45–57.

Hsu, Kai-yu. "The Poems of Li Ch'ing-chao (1084–1141)," *PMLA*, 77 (1962), 521–528.

Hu, Pin-ching. *Li Ching-chao*. New York, 1966.

Lin, Yu-t'ang. *The Gay Genius; The Life and Times of Su Tungpo*. New York, 1947.

Liu, James J. Y. *Major Lyricists of the Northern Sung, 960–1126*. Princeton, 1974.

Lo, Irving Yucheng. *Hsin Ch'i-chi*. New York, 1971.

Whitaker, K. P. K. "Some Notes on the Tsyr," *Bulletin of the School of Oriental and African Studies*, 14 (1952), 115–138.

YÜAN SONGS

Goodrich, L. Carrington. "Western Regions Writers of Chinese Lyrics during the Yüan," *Transactions*, International Conference of Orientalists in Japan, / (1962), 17–21.

Liu, Chun-jo. "Some Observations on the Parallel Structure in Ma Chih-yüan's Hsiao-Ling (short lyrics)," *Tsing Hua Journal of Chinese Studies*, VII.2 (1969), 67–91.

Schlepp, Wayne. *San-ch'ü, Its Technique and Imagery*. Madison, Milwaukee, and London, 1970.

Wai-lim Yip is Professor of Literature at the University of California at San Diego.

Library of Congress Cataloging-in-Publication Data
Chinese poetry: an anthology of major modes and genres/Wai-lim Yip.
Originally published: Berkeley: University of California Press, 1976.
Includes bibliographical references.
ISBN 0-8223-1951-9 (cloth: alk. paper). —ISBN 0-8223-1946-2 (pbk.: alk. paper)
1. Chinese poetry—Translations into English. I. Yip, Wai-lim.
PL2658.E3C58   1997   895.1'1008—dc20   96-36662 CIP